ORPHANS OF THE SEA

Ken Jones

ORPHANS OF THE SEA

HARVILL PRESS, LONDON

ISBN 0 00 272604 1

© Ken Jones 1970

Printed in Great Britain by Collins
Clear-Type Press, London and Glasgow,
for the publishers The Harvill Press Limited,
30a Pavilion Road, London SW1.

To Mary and Linda

Acknowledgements

I wish to thank all those who supplied photographs which have been used to illustrate this book. In particular:
Bob Salmon, Plymouth, Devon;
Richards Brothers, Penzance;
J. H. Bottrell, Penzance;
Ken Young, St Agnes;
Roy Hughes, St Austell;
The Sunday Mirror.
My grateful thanks also to:
Mr Griffiths of the R.S.P.C.A., Penzance, for his great efforts at the time of the Seal Disaster and for his continued interest in our work;
Mr Gardner, Chief Inspector, R.S.P.C.A., Truro Branch, for his help and assistance;
Veterinary Surgeons: Mr Greene of Newquay, whose advice has been invaluable; Messrs Hill and Littleton of Truro for their quick attention and patience in treatment;
The Seal Research Unit, Lowestoft, Suffolk, in particular Mr Nigel Bonner and his assistant who have shown great interest in the Sanctuary and who are supplying vital information;
Miss Hilda Bamber of B.B.C. Television, Plymouth, who brought the work of the Seal Sanctuary to the attention of a wide public;
The *Birmingham Post* and their readers, many of whom sent donations and encouraging letters;
The staff and children from schools in Cornwall, Cambridge, the Midlands and Holland, who by their activities raised funds to help seals in distress;

ACKNOWLEDGEMENTS

British Cod Liver Oils (Hull and Grimsby) Ltd. for donations of their 'Super Solvitax Cod Liver Oil' used in the treatment of seals;

And last but not least, our good friend and neighbour, Miss Beams Burdett, who has shown her devotion to seals on many occasions, helping with their feeding and in the Sanctuary generally.

My special thanks to Sir William Collins for his interest and encouragement.

It is impossible to acknowledge everyone individually who has given help or shown interest in our work for seals, but our thanks go out to them and we promise to continue to do our best to give life to the Orphans of the Sea.

Contents

	INTRODUCTION	13
1	How we became involved with Seals	17
2	Sammy	23
3	Simon	29
4	Sally – A victim of the *Torrey Canyon*	35
5	Intruders	46
6	A Double Tragedy	53
7	Sea-Lions in the Sanctuary	62
8	Simon II and Sally II	66
9	The Suffering that People can cause	71
10	A Disastrous Winter	77
11	Protection for the Wild Life of our Coasts	91

List of Illustrations

between pages 24 *and* 25
The beach at St Agnes
The Seal Sanctuary
Rescue of a seal pup
Pup being fed by tube

between pages 40 *and* 41
Simon I looking for me
Simon I being X-rayed

between pages 56 *and* 57
Sally II meets new pup
Sally II and Simon II
The sea-lions Kim and Judy
Baby seals hardening off in their new homes

between pages 72 *and* 73
Oiled guillemots
Blacky's body showing burn marks
Seals' playtime
Badger

Introduction

BRITAIN has a very large population of Atlantic seals. Seventy-five per cent live off the Scottish coast; the seal population in Cornwall and the Scilly Islands is much smaller, probably because the little coves which once made ideal breeding grounds are now used by holiday makers. In their new breeding grounds, usually at the base of the cliffs, they are safe from men but not from the rollers of the Atlantic.

Breeding takes place between September and November, but odd pups are born up to early spring. Though their breeding grounds are inaccessible to man, nature is not kind to the seals at this time of year. Gale force north-westerly winds blow and powerful waves pound the cliffs and, at Spring Tides, the seas reach the breeding grounds and wash the pups out. Those newly born are weak, their fur is of thick white wool which absorbs water and becomes heavy, making it difficult for the pups to ride the waves. The mothers do not stay all the time with their babies, they often feed them at high-tide and then go out to sea returning on the next tide to give them another meal. But in the interval the pups may have been washed a few miles down the coast line thus making it impossible for the mothers to find them. Moreover, in bad weather, the pups may have been smashed against the rocks so that by the time the luckier ones reach the shore, they are often injured, exhausted and starving and suffer from lung congestion and pneumonia. These are the pups we rescue and care for and for which we have built the Sanctuary.

In cases where all goes well the mothers feed the pups for two to three weeks. They usually weigh about thirty pounds at birth, then while being suckled, they blow up like balloons and by the time they are ready to be weaned they weigh up to 120 or 130 pounds. Now they are deserted and need to live on their blubber, built up by the mother's rich milk, until they are able to feed on fish.

Seals existed long before man; in those days they were land mammals, later they took to the sea, but they still need to surface for air. They have a small brain but their intelligence is remarkable though, as with people, it varies in degree; they are always alert, listening, on the watch. There is no doubt that they can communicate with each other (though we do not yet know much about the way in which they do this), and we can, with patience, get them to understand certain of our words.

As to the rate at which their intelligence develops, from our observations, pups notice and listen but have very little reaction to what is going on. It is not till they are two or three years old that their individual intelligence begins to show. And, after all, it is at about that age that a human baby starts to learn. Very soon they get to know their names, and their feed and play times.

Seals have an acute sense of smell and their sense of direction is outstanding. A totally blind seal has been known to find its pup, to go to and from the sea and to catch fish. There is no doubt that their eyesight is excellent, this is proved by the way in which seagulls fascinate them and the amount of time they devote, in the summer, to fly catching. To do this they lift a large part of their body out of the water and move like dolphins to attack their prey, which, more often than not they miss. They also react to seeing themselves in a mirror. Sometimes it scares them. They do not react to electric light but torches frighten them.

A seal's hearing is good and they seem very sensitive to vibration. At one time the local council renewed the water mains down to our beach. This involved drilling the rock three feet deep for two or three hundred yards. While the work was going on the seals were very restless and shook their heads continually as if picking up the vibrations from the water, but when I emptied the pool they seemed still more upset, so I refilled it.

We do not know whether they have a sense of taste. They have saliva but they swallow without chewing. What we do know is the rapidity with which they digest their food. An hour after taking ten or fourteen pounds of fish their stomach may be empty. The fish is eaten whole and possibly the head helps the process of digestion. It is believed that a mixed diet of mackerel, herrings and whiting would be good for them but my seals won't touch whiting.

Scratching themselves is one of the seals' great occupations. They draw the flat side of their front flipper from the top of their head slowly over their eyes and nostrils, then they open their mouths and bite the flipper, rather like a baby sucking its thumb.

Their back flippers stretch and open wide like webs; often a seal will twist them round each other and then curl them up. They do this especially when they are tired and ready for sleep. Sometimes they take a long while to get comfortable, twisting one way and the other and resting their heads against a wall or the floor. They sleep on their sides, and occasionally on their backs, but very rarely on their tummies.

In recent years, seals have had a lot of publicity. That people should take an interest in them is nothing new; long ago, in some parts of the world, they were worshipped as gods; what is new is that, whereas in the past they were killed for food by such hard living people as Eskimos, they are now killed to satisfy man's greed for wealth and luxury.

It is sickening to read of the present inhuman killings of baby seals, clubbed to death in front of their mothers. As the story I am about to tell proves, seals have a deep affection for each other and the seal mothers undoubtedly feel the suffering of their newly born pups.

In this book I have tried to describe our efforts to save the lives of injured and abandoned baby seals and the trust and affection they have shown us.

CHAPTER ONE

How we became involved with Seals

I WAS born in 1926 at Tonypandy in the Rhondda Valley, South Wales. My father had been incapacitated by injuries he had received in the First World War and so I had to leave my Secondary School early and take a job down the mines to support the family. When my father died, at the age of forty-two, I became the breadwinner. As a small child I was always bringing home stray and injured animals and although times were so bad, my parents were sympathetic and never discouraged me.

At the age of twenty I left Wales for the Midlands and joined the staff of Burntwood Hospital as a trainee nurse. It was in Staffordshire that I met my wife; then, because we were both eager to get married, I left the hospital for a better paid job in the Cannock mines. I now studied to become a mining engineer, and after a few years, had progressed to the status of an Official of the National Coal Board. In 1960, owing to the closure of many of the old mines and the effects of a bad accident and illness, I decided to invest my savings in a beach café at St Agnes. As soon as I had settled in Cornwall I joined the Civil Defence, Auxiliary Coastguard Watch and Cliff Rescue services.

My wife had very much the same childhood as I; she too was born in 1926, her father died early and she was left with her mother and younger brother to support. Like me she loved animals. In the early days of our marriage she helped me in my studies and to-day gives me the greatest support in my work in the Sanctuary. Our daughter Linda was born in 1953; she too is a great animal lover.

St Agnes is a pretty little bay situated between Perranporth and Porthtowan, twelve miles from Newquay on the one side and twenty-five miles from St Ives on the other.

Our café is in Trevaunance Cove, to reach it you go through the quaint little village and down a valley of green grass and trees. We live just above the sea overlooking the beach, with views across to Perranporth and Newquay, and the fine rugged coastline that is typical of Cornwall. Our bungalow when we bought it was surrounded by lawns; little did we think then that all these lawns would disappear and a 'Seal Sanctuary' develop to take their place. Coming from the Midlands the sea meant little to us, only very rarely had we seen it, and we didn't even know that seals existed.

Looking back over ten years we wonder how we were led to this small Cornish cove and to a life which neither of us could have foreseen in our wildest dreams. It must have been the hand of fate that decided us on buying the small beach business, because, but for this, we would not have been on the spot when our first orphan of the sea came into our bay looking for help.

She was a creamy white furry bundle, three feet long and weighing about thirty pounds. Her umbilical cord was newly cut which meant that she was only a day or two old. Many people gathered around the pup, some dogs were also interested and it was getting frightened. We left the café and went down to the bottom of the cliff. The little seal snarled as we came near. Our first instinct was to get it back to sea in case the dogs should attack it, so we got behind it and the pup started flapping across the beach; this was what we wanted it to do. Already it had cut its eye from being washed against the rocks. When it was about thirty yards away from the cliff, we pushed it into the sea, but back it came. We repeated this operation many times until finally we decided to take the pup up to our bungalow for safety.

Several visitors followed us and we got them to carry some sea water to fill our bath. This shows you how much knowledge we had of seals. We were sure the pup must be kept in water or it would die. When the bath was full we put the little seal into it. All went well for a few seconds, then there was splashing and suddenly the water went down the plughole and the pup lay in the empty bath looking sorry for itself. I decided I needed help and rang the nearest zoo and several animal societies to find out what I ought to do. After many telephone calls, I was told to put the pup back to sea, near to Seal Cove, which was the seals' breeding ground.

The boat was launched and we went to Seal Cove, where we threw the pup overboard, thinking it would swim away; instead it tried to climb back into the boat. We kept pushing it away, finally it swam off, and we went back to the beach. We were sitting down, smoking and laughing about our experiences, when in came a passer-by to tell us that the seal was back on the beach.

Down we went, and there it was, the same pup looking up at us with its beautiful, big, pleading eyes, as if it were saying 'Don't do that again, I need help.' I picked it up and carried it into an old caravan in our garden. I am sure the pup thought I was her mother; whichever way I moved, she followed me. The poor thing must have been starving, so we now had to find out how to feed her and what to feed her on. Again, I made many telephone calls but got no information, until finally we were told to give her twelve ounces of margarine to one pint of milk four times a day. We were warned that more than likely we would need to force feed by a tube into the pup's stomach. The son of a friend of ours was a doctor, and he very kindly came down to show us how to do this.

When he did it it looked easy, so for the next feed we mixed the margarine and milk, and went quite confidently to the caravan. I held the pup and tried to open its jaws to put the tube down, but there was nothing doing. At first I could not move its jaws at all, but finally, I managed to force a little opening, and my wife pushed the tube through; as she did so, down came the seal's small teeth on to the tube. Again I forced its jaws open and Mary pushed the tube down, then she poured the milk into the funnel. Nothing happened, no milk was going down, the pup's teeth were again clenching the tube, so now I had to keep its jaws open until all the milk was down. Mary then pulled the tube out, and that was our first feed done. The pup gave a few hiccups but seemed contented. Mary took the feeding apparatus to the bungalow for sterilising before the next feed. We knew that cleanliness was as essential for a seal pup as for a human baby. I stayed with Cindy, as we called her, and gave her a little fuss; she appreciated this and sucked at my hand for comfort.

The weather was so warm and sunny that after giving her a few more feeds, we took Cindy out on to the lawn. Being inquisitive, she first nosed around, then she came to my feet. I lay down on the lawn and she crawled onto my chest, sniffing at my face and scratching me with her hand-like flipper. She had no fear of me and pawed just like a dog asking to play. I trusted Cindy and she trusted me. I tickled her tummy, which she enjoyed, opening her mouth as if laughing and asking for more. On land it is difficult for a seal to play with a ball, but Cindy was soon scratching at one and trying to bite it.

I used to talk silly talk to her as if I were playing with a baby. She loved it and would turn her head to one side, as though she understood what I was saying. After playing for a while we took her back to the caravan for a rest, after all, she was only a baby and food and rest were the main essentials for her. Occasionally I popped in to keep her company. She seemed quite happy with the quantity of milk we were giving her. But we had read that seal pups wean themselves at three to four weeks old, so when she was approaching that age, I rang up some fishermen at St Ives to order fish for her.

It was a Friday, and Cindy's fish was due to be delivered on the following day. I went into the caravan and greeted her, but she showed no interest. Thinking she was tired I left her to rest. We prepared the last feed of milk, the next one would be the fish, and took it to the caravan. Still she showed no interest. As, however, she had been having regular meals missing one would not matter much.

Next morning I got up early to see how she was. I went to the caravan and found her lying quite still in the corner. Thinking she must be fast asleep, I called out to her. When I did this she usually threw up her head quickly, but this time nothing happened. I crept up to her and went to tickle her tummy, she was stiff, she was dead. I could not believe it, tears came into my eyes,

I gave her artificial respiration, but I could see it was too late. What had I done wrong? Why had this happened?

I sat there for quite a while, then I thought I must break the news to Mary, and to Linda who had helped with Cindy and loved her as I did. I went back to the bungalow, to the kitchen where Mary was working and stood and looked at her for a moment, then the sad news had to be told. Mary asked the same question I was asking myself: what had we done wrong for this to happen after four weeks?

I rang the vet and told him that I wanted a post mortem. After it had been done we were informed that the margarine in the milk had proved too much for the pup to absorb. We had been given the wrong advice, we had lost Cindy through lack of knowledge. We determined to read all the books we could find on the grey seal, then, should another pup come ashore for help, we would know what to do and there would not be another tragedy. However, very little information on the feeding of pups seemed to be available, for only in recent years have any surveys, or scientific research, been done on grey seals.

CHAPTER TWO

Sammy

OUR second seal was washed in one month later. It had lost its white coat, was about four weeks old and very thin and exhausted. If it had not been so thin, I would not have taken it from the beach, as, after all, the sea was its home.

I carried it up to the caravan and put it down to rest for a while. A few hours later, I went to see how it was. As I opened the door, it came at me like a wild bull, showing its full set of sharp teeth. I closed the door, but was still able to see it through the wire netting I had put on the top half. Then I walked back, and told Mary how affectionate our new arrival was. Nevertheless, it was necessary to get fish quickly and try to feed it, so I went to the nearest fishmonger's and bought some sprats.

Carrying the fish we both approached the caravan. I opened the door and asked Mary to hold it ajar in case I needed to make a quick retreat. Then, slowly, I walked towards what looked to me like a vicious lion. I was waving a sprat in the air and gradually getting closer to it. Suddenly the seal's neck seemed to stretch out to at least two feet, I nearly lost my fingers, and the sprat was tossed across the caravan. Another quick movement from the seal and I was back through the door.

We had to find some other way of feeding our new patient. I got a stick, made a slit in the end and put a sprat into it. The seal snapped at the sprat and threw it to one side: we tried again, this time it chewed at it, and down it went. We did this with quite a few sprats, and luckily the pup ate most of them; we decided to repeat this manoeuvre four times a day.

The following morning we braved the pup, opening the door of the caravan so that we could feed it by hand. By now we were dressed for the part: wellington boots, thick jackets and gloves. Bravely I went inside, again Mary held the door open ready for a quick escape. I took the fish, a mackerel, by its tail, this at least left the length of the fish between the seal's teeth and my hand. He took it with a snatch, but not so viciously as before. Quickly I got more fish ready, and without being chewed or tasted, they went down. But when there were none left, the pup came snarling at me. I passed Mary like a sprinter, she closed the door quickly, and we sighed with relief. At least our orphan, whom we named Sampson, had had a good meal.

Things went on very much the same way for the next few days, and gradually the pup put on weight. We thought we would give it four more days – ten days in all, after that he should be able to fend for himself.

On the Saturday afternoon we took Sampson back to the beach he had come in on, put him on the water's edge, and off he went. Only twice did his head pop up, as if to say 'Thank you', and that was the last we saw of him. At least we had fattened him up a little, given him strength and weaned him on to fish, so making it possible for him to survive at sea.

In its natural life, a pup's mother leaves it after about three weeks. Swallowing a fish for the first time often proves a difficulty. Some pups do not understand what they have to do and therefore die of starvation. But the

The beach of St Agnes

Seal Sanctuary next to the beach café

Rescue of a seal pup

Pup gaining confidence after being fed by tube

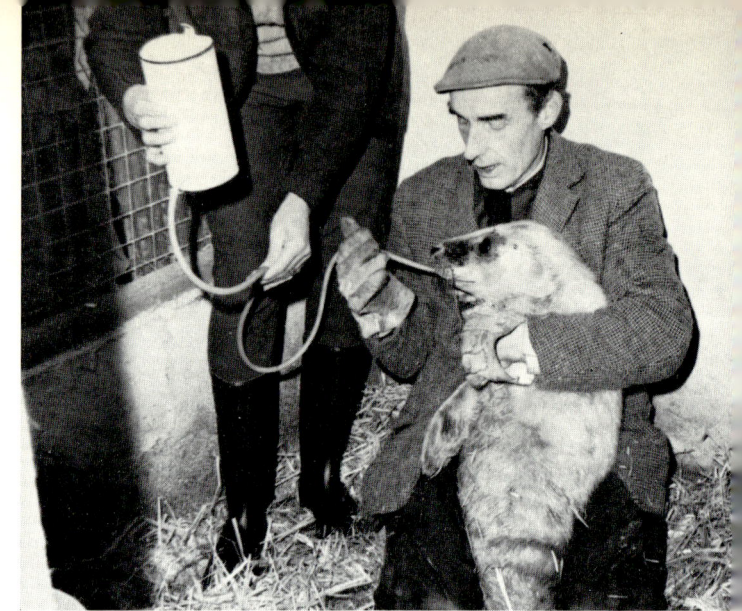

majority usually wean themselves in time, and having developed a thick layer of fat from the mother's rich milk, they have a period of a few weeks, living on this fat, in which to learn how to feed themselves.

It was in September of the following year that Sammy the seal was washed in. After getting a telephone call, we put a clothes basket in the back of the car, in order to make it easier to carry the pup off the beach. We were expecting a gentle furry white pup which would not cause much trouble, but when we arrived we found it had shed three parts of its coat, had some nasty cuts on its head and body, and its nostrils were thick with mucus which made its breathing very bad. As we approached it snarled and waved its flipper.

I grabbed hold of its back flippers and gently pulled it into the basket, putting a blanket over it to prevent it from getting out. We took it straight to the vet for treatment, then put the basket on the back seat and Mary sat with it, in case it should decide to get out. We did not want to end up in the ditch, so I told Mary to shout if it got restless and I'd stop the car. Once or twice it tried to leave its basket, but we got home safely.

For this pup we used one of the chalets on the beach, there was more room there, and we thought the sound of the sea might make it feel at home. Owing to its condition and also its age (two to three weeks) we thought we should give it milk for a week and then wean it on to fish. So we were back again to the tube, but by now we had a better idea of what quantity we should give and what fat content to add.

As usual we sterilised the equipment. We gave the milk luke warm in six feeds a day; the pup put up quite a struggle when first we tried to get the tube down, but we succeeded and after five days we decided to put it on to fish.

Sammy slept on a bed of straw, which was cleaned out regularly (the straw was to prove fatal later on).

This time for weaning the pup on to fish, I held him while Mary dropped the fish into his mouth. It stuck to his top jaw, and we had to use a smooth stick to push it to the back of his throat to get him to swallow. However, after a few unsuccessful tries, he took to his new diet, and finally fed without the need for a stick.

After that we took a large bowl of sprats to him four times a day. Mary would hold the bowl and hand a sprat at a time to me and I gave them to him. Occasionally he would throw one out on to the straw, and if I picked it up, he would snap at my hand, so I let it lie there. As soon as we came to the last few sprats, we had to get ready to get out of the door quickly for, as with Sampson, Sammy went for one when he saw there was no more food going.

I'll never forget one particular evening; as the nights were dark we used what was supposed to be a hurricane lamp to light our way. The wind was howling, and as we went down the hill to the chalet we covered the lamp, but still the flame kept on flickering. We arrived at the door of the chalet, Mary holding the bowl of fish and I the lamp. When we opened it the light went out. Sammy snarled, and we heard his flip-flop coming towards us; not being able to see him, we made the quickest ever getaway, but still the flip-flop kept following us. I hurriedly relit the lamp and went round the other side of the chalet, taking a few sprats with me. Now I saw Sammy and came up to him and showed him the fish, he turned round and followed me back into the chalet. He still dropped some fish, usually those whose heads were torn. Very often he'd later pick them up and eat them complete with pieces of straw. He did so now, but we didn't think much about it at the time.

Soon came another call; a seal had been found in very bad condition, those who had discovered it said they would bring it over to us. When they arrived, they told us that they had put it in the boot of the car, and after travelling about a mile, one of them noticed that the boot was open, and stopping the car they discovered that the seal had gone, so they went back and after half a mile they found it on the grass, well off the road and no worse for its adventure. This time they put it inside the car.

I helped them to get it out and we put it into the caravan. It was a male pup, about three to four weeks old, obviously it had congestion of the lungs, and it too was very thin. Its head was beautiful, but its eyes were not bright, for they were thick with a yellow secretion. I bathed the pup's eyes and put some lotion into the lids. We called him Simon and we let him rest for a few hours.

We decided to wean Simon on sprats, since they were smaller and easier to swallow. He did not snap at me when I caught hold of him to give him the fish, and I opened his jaws, using gloves. At first he seemed to have some difficulty in swallowing, but he soon got the idea and we were able to give him a good feed but we took care not to overload him.

Later, we had him injected, and obtained an antibiotic which we gave him twice a day in the fish. As sprats are very small, which makes it difficult to put powder into them, we tried him with a small mackerel. First we gave it without the powder, pushing the fish down his throat; he took it fairly easily. The next fish I slit and put the required dose inside it. Simon didn't notice the difference.

I did not like keeping him in the caravan, so I bought a second-hand wooden shed and placed it on the lawn at the side of the garage. The first few days he ate well, but his breathing was very bad and I took care to keep him very warm. I also made a wire netting run in front of the shed, so that, later on, I could bring him out into the sunshine.

In the meantime, Sammy seemed to be improving, but he did not put on much weight. The vet gave me another powder to put into his fish and we added cod liver oil and some extra vitamins. Unfortunately, owing to our lack of experience we did not recognise the signs or symptoms of what was happening to Sammy. Worried about him, we took him up to the garden and put him near Simon.

It was now that I started to build my first small pool. Since I had found that the seals were best weaned on to fish as soon as possible, I thought I must teach them to eat fish in the water, as they would have to do at sea.

The following day Sammy died. The post mortem showed straw in his stomach blocking the intestines. We learned by these sad experiences and they were never repeated. As a result a good many of the pups we rescued are now safely in the ocean.

It was a sad blow to us losing Sammy, we had given him a lot of our time. When a fish fell on the straw he must have picked it up after we had left him and each time he had eaten the straw as well. Future seals were never fed near straw, and any fish that fell on the floor we removed before we left.

CHAPTER THREE

Simon

SIMON, whose ribs we could see when he came to us, was fattening slowly. I let him out on a warm day into the netting run, he enjoyed this. I went in to dinner, Simon was sleeping outside, all looked well. Twenty minutes later there was a knock at the door, then a man came in and told us that Simon was fifty yards up the road outside the local pub. I went running up, there he was having a look round, perhaps he was feeling thirsty and wanted a quick one?

He let me pick him up. He was getting quite heavy now. I took him back to his shed and secured the netting he had wriggled under so there would be no fear of his disappearing again. As I was fixing the netting he looked sadly at me. I think he wanted some attention so I started playing with him, tickling him on the tummy, and under his chin.

I carried on with the pool, occasionally spending a little time with Simon. It looked as if his lungs were permanently damaged and he would never go back to the sea, so the quicker I could finish the pool the better for him. I worked day and night, and when I had put the final touches to it, I bought some wooden fencing to put round the pool, for two reasons: to keep Simon in, and also to act as a shield against the winds.

When the concrete had hardened off, I filled it with water. We were excited to know what Simon's reactions would be when he went into the pool for the first time. I had made a gradual slope to it, only six feet from where Simon was resting.

Now I removed the netting with which I had covered the pool while the concrete was still soft. Simon just lay where he was for a few minutes so I went to the other end of the pool and waited. Then he lifted himself up and started to come towards me. It had been raining, the concrete at the side of the pool was smooth and wet, he began to slide and splash – he was in the pool. The water level was six inches below the top of the concrete; Simon tried to get out but kept sliding back. Now I threw a coloured ball into the pool, he swam towards it, then pounced on it and the ball flew up into the air. He did this a few times then, lying on his back, he came to the side. I tickled his tummy, he loved this and kept on smacking his chest asking for more. I was still not sure about how he might use his teeth. I stroked his head but as I did so he tried to grab hold of my hand. I let him hold my sleeve, it soon started to unravel, so I put on a glove and took the risk of his teeth biting through it. He pressed hard at first, I think, in excitement, then he caught hold of the finger tips of the glove and pulled it off. I thought, here goes, and put my hand to his nose, he opened his mouth, I could see his teeth glistening; he caught hold of my hand and closed his mouth, not hard, but just hard enough to leave teeth marks. I kept talking to him and gradually he eased his teeth off. After that I could tickle his tongue and do as I wished.

He had a wonderful temperament. He would start to show off by nosing the ball, then he would pounce out of the pool; when on land he would wriggle his body, move his head backwards and forwards teasing me and trying to get me to play. I would kneel and pretend I was taking no notice of him; then he would crawl towards me and nudge my arm with his nose. Still I would take no notice and he would scratch me with his flipper, after this, if he got no response, he would roll on his back making grunting noises. At this point I *had* to play with him. After a while I would push him into the pool, but no sooner was he in than he would pop out again. I noticed that his breathing was very hard, whenever he chased me, he gasped, like a person with a heavy cold. He was now well over 120 pounds and when he rested his weight on my feet I could not move. If I tried, he would grab hold of my trousers, and I'd be less one leg of my trousers if I continued to endeavour to escape. Simon could move quite fast over a short distance, his body lifting up and slapping down on the concrete.

Many people came to see the Sanctuary. This gave Simon the chance to show off when I was not there. Sometimes, when he was fast asleep under water, only very occasionally coming up for air, people would arrive at my door saying he was dead.

I put a hose-pipe connected to a tap into the pool, Simon would wrap this hose around himself thus supporting his body and would often go to sleep in this position.

I was still working just outside the fencing of the pool and sometimes Simon, using his flippers, would loosen two strips of wood, it was interlaced fencing, and pop his head through to see what was going on.

That winter three more pups were washed in and another two found dead. As the procedure is much the same with all the pups (except that each has his own personality), I shall write mainly about the ones that will always be remembered by us and also by the many thousands of visitors who came to the Sanctuary.

The three new pups were successfully weaned on to fish and returned to the sea. One was with us only four days, another a week, the third eleven days.

During the summer months I could not give Simon very much of my time, but a neighbour who took an interest in the work we were doing and who was attracted to Simon, used to come and play with him, and if I could not go to the pool when it was his feeding time, she would feed him for me. Of course, I came along as soon as I could; when I reached the gate out he would jump from the pool, and behave like a dog would if you'd been out for the day, flapping across towards me, putting his teeth around my jacket, then trying to climb on to my back. If I had my cap on that would be the first thing he would go for, taking it off my head. He was now devoted to me and if he had had his way he would never have let me out of the pen.

On one occasion Mary and I had to leave the Sanctuary for a few days owing to her mother's illness. We arranged for a neighbour to feed the seals and care for them, and every night I telephoned to hear how they were doing. When we returned Simon behaved just as some dogs do when their owners have left them for a while. As soon as I reached the car park I looked down at him and shouted to him, usually when he heard my voice he would be out of the pool in a jiffy but now he just looked reproachfully at me. I went down to the pool to talk to him but he ignored me and when I tried to stroke his head he went off to the other side of the pool. It took me

SIMON

nearly ten days to get him out of his fit of sulks and back to our normal relationship.

In July, Simon started having lung congestion again. I put an antibiotic into his fish but the following day he was worse, so I rang the vet to give him an injection and I emptied the pool to make it easier to get hold of him. But, although we were great friends, Simon at once sensed that something untoward was going on as soon as the vet jumped into the pool. I held him tight round the neck and told the vet to inject quickly. Simon was not at all pleased about this, so, after it was over, I let him rest in the empty pool to give him a chance to recover from what must have been an embarrassing situation for him.

That night I myself jumped into the pool and talked to him for half an hour. By then he had got over the injection, so we were friends again. I left the pool empty that night, letting him rest, as the weather was good, and in a few days Simon was back to normal. He ate well, in fact, by September, I was worried about his size; the weight he was carrying was considerable for a weak-chested seal and I gradually cut down his food, even so, he was eating fourteen pounds of fish a day.

Simon was a great favourite especially with children who, before going home, would come to say 'Goodbye' and 'See you next year, Simon, take care of yourself'. Even old people came on the last day of their holiday to bid him farewell.

I had just closed the shop for the end of the season when the first pup of the year came in. He was the usual creamy white, furry bundle. We used the wooden shed that Simon had at first been in. We were more experienced now in handling and feeding, so it seemed much easier.

We kept the pup clear of Simon as we thought it would not be fair to let them get used to each other when they would have to be parted in a few weeks' time, supposing that the pup was returned to the sea. This pup was no problem, but the one we got two weeks later died the following morning, though he had been injected for pneumonia.

He may have been on the beach for days and in that case was past the stage at which any treatment could do him any good. Most of those we found that winter were either injured or had been separated from their mothers by gales. All the same, it was a successful winter for us; only that one pup died, and not through our fault as we had received him too late.

CHAPTER FOUR

Sally – A victim of the Torrey Canyon

DURING Easter week, 1967, the *Torrey Canyon* went adrift on the Seven Stone Rocks off Land's End. Attempts were made to pull her off, but gradually she started to break in two and the Government decided to blow her up as there were thousands of gallons of oil aboard and already slicks of oil had reached our beaches. The sea birds were hit hard: they were coming in on nearly every beach in Cornwall. Centres were set up for cleaning them. At first, as I've said, we started attending to them on our own beaches, but owing to the numbers involved and also to the considerable time we were spending in collecting them, it seemed better to take them to the nearest cleaning centre, which was at Perranporth. We were out all day and all night. In the evening we switched the headlights of the car on so that they lit up the beach, and we collected many birds this way. We also got many a soaking for it was easy to trip over stones or large rocks and go sprawling into the sea. The beaches were thick with oil: it was a horrible feeling just walking through it while the poor birds were suffocating in it.

There was an uproar for holidaymakers would soon be arriving and nearly every beach was plastered with oil. As fast as we moved the oil off by filling trucks and dumping it into an old mine shaft near the beach, more oil came in and the coves were as bad as ever. Later, troops, the Fire Brigades and members of the Civil

Defence Force all worked to clear the beaches with detergents and besides that, many people helped, giving up their time to try and save the birds. Nevertheless, thousands died.

A rough calculation suggests that as a result of the disaster, over ten thousand birds died. Despite all the work involved in catching and cleaning them, very few survived. Indeed I think it is a question whether badly oiled birds should not be destroyed immediately, instead of being left to suffer over a prolonged period.

Birds covered in oil cannot fly and therefore battle with the sea; they become weak, their feathers are soaked and they suffer from shock. When, finally, they reach the rocks or the beach, we add to their strain by chasing them, even though we do it in good faith, trying to save their lives. After this they are placed in a dark box, which adds to their distress. Then they are carted around, other birds being put in with them, and sometimes fighting with them. When they arrive at their destination, their feathers are rubbed with solutions intended to clean off the oil; finally they are placed in front of fan heaters. All this is unnatural, and, I think, in most cases, proves too much for the bird. The dilemma is that if we do not try and save some, then we may lose our entire population of sea birds. What is the answer? Should we try to save all of them, thereby perhaps causing further suffering to many, or try to save only the lightly oiled birds and put the rest out of their misery, or should we destroy all the oiled birds? The only satisfactory answer would, I think, be a dry powder which would destroy the oil without the bird having to be washed; such a powder would need to be applied as soon as the victim is caught, and I

SALLY – A VICTIM OF THE TORREY CANYON

believe a lot is being done to try and invent something of the sort.

Every time we went on rescue expeditions it seemed that the winds howled and rain poured down! We covered every possible place from Perranporth to Godrevy. No one wants to see another *Torrey Canyon*, but who can tell? The tankers now being built are bigger; errors can be made by the skipper or crew.

While this was going on, I was also getting phone calls about seals in difficulty, and I think I covered the whole of Cornwall in answering them. Most of the seals were, in fact, all right, but as they were swimming in slicks of oil, watch had to be kept in case their eyes were affected. To check the situation properly we formed a cliff party: ropes and harnesses were loaded into a jeep and a search of the coastline was organised. There were five of us in all – none too many – since one or two of us might need to be lowered down the cliffs for a seal rescue operation. We had many a frightening experience whilst being lowered, but all of us were good men on the ropes so the only horrid thought was 'What if the rope were to break?' We did however get one seal who had been blinded by the oil. She was a female, we called her Sally. She was plastered in oil and it took some time to remove it. There was not much we could do about her eyes, one was completely gone, and the other had only blurred vision.

We put Sally into the shed near the pool, washed off most of the oil, treated the eyes and let her settle down. The poor little thing was going to need a lot of care and comfort.

Sally was at the weaning age so we put her straight on to fish. Probably because her sight was poor she was very nervous and attacked anything that touched her, including me. We had to be very careful when handling her. I think she knew we were trying to help her, but she wasn't having any fuss, so, as soon as she was fed, out we got. The blind eye was healing but the other had a white mist over it and still looked sore. She also had a nasty scar on her side, but we were assured this would soon heal.

Simon had started throwing his head back when he was swimming, I thought perhaps a fish bone had stuck in his throat and would probably loosen itself in time. But as he kept on doing this for days, I began to wonder whether he had some sort of infection in his gullet. My vet called to examine him and we decided to X-ray him. The nearest vet who had the right equipment was at Exeter, so we contacted his office and made the necessary arrangements. The pool was emptied and my own vet came to inject Simon hoping to put him to sleep. The maximum dose was given so that by the time the X-ray unit arrived he should have been asleep. But, in fact, when they came Simon was only a little dozey. We tried to put the X-ray unit by him but he snarled and snapped. So that he should not get too distressed I went down to reassure him, and gently held his head.

The unit was then brought in and slowly placed over him. He did not like the machine and I had difficulty in holding him. However, in the end, a few X-rays were taken. It took nearly a week before we got the result, which was negative. There was no fish bone stuck in his throat. We therefore treated him as for an infection. After two weeks he stopped throwing his head back, and that was another worry over.

Sally, in the meantime, was slowly improving as to

health, but not as to temperament. She would still snap when I tried to touch her. She didn't mind people getting close to her, but she did not like anyone touching her.

I decided to build another pool at the side of the existing one. This would enable me to wean future pups in a pool of their own, away from Simon. I made a start but was not left alone for long. First Simon put his head in the hole I had dug, then he grabbed my sleeve and pulled me away.

Very soon, I let Sally into the netting run. This made Simon inquisitive; out he came to sniff at her. She was not very keen on this proceeding, gave a cry and shook her flipper. Simon, being good natured, did not take too much notice of her hostile attitude and just slithered back into his pool, occasionally coming up to the side, and popping his head up to see what she was up to.

When I had finished the new pool, I put some netting to divide the two and then let Sally into hers.

In the water Sally looked a pathetic figure. Her one eye completely gone, the other one white, but all the same, she had a sweet face. After a few days I decided to take down the netting between the two pools and see how Simon and Sally would react to each other.

At first neither of the seals attempted to go close to the other. Sally's pool was a little higher than Simon's, with a smooth concrete slope down. It had been raining and all the surrounds were wet. As I went in, Sally jumped out of her pool, and in doing so slid down the slope into Simon's pool.

There was quite a scuffle, mainly I think because Simon had been caught unawares. Then they sniffed at each other and afterwards Sally swam away, with Simon sniffing her back. I dared not leave them yet for if they didn't get on, Sally would have to go back to her own pool. I need not have worried, they got on beautifully. Simon kept his flippers round her: he thought she was wonderful. His face was mottled brown now, at first it had been mottled dark grey.

It was spring, the sun was shining, and both seals spent most of their time basking in the sun. I then noticed light specks coming out on the bald patches of Simon's skin (he had lost most of his fur some time earlier), and in a few days I realised he was growing a new coat. It felt soft and silky and it seemed no time at all before he had a coat as beautiful as the one he had when he was washed in. I think Sally fancied him all the more now that he no longer looked like a tramp.

On one occasion, when I went in to feed them, Simon was missing. I searched everywhere, there was no opening in the fencing; he could not have got out, I couldn't understand it. Then I heard a sneeze behind the shed which was against the back wall. (The shed was raised up on blocks and planks as it had a wooden floor.) There was a drop behind it and there was Simon, wedged between the wall and the bottom of the shed. He was not hurt, but, fat as he was, he could not move. He looked at me as if he were saying, 'Aren't I a right nit'. I could not move him an inch, finally I had to cut a hole in the back of the shed near his head and let him get out that way.

I had a rockery built up in stages, each stage about three feet high with a platform between each layer. One day I found Simon on the second layer stretched out and enjoying the sun. I held a fish to him to entice him down, but he didn't respond. He was scared stiff. He had got there by climbing, but, with his figure, getting down was going

Simon I looking for me . . .

... wanting to play

Simon I being X-rayed

to be a problem. I climbed up and put my back just beneath him hoping he might use it as a stepping stone, but he was evidently too afraid of falling, so I fetched two long thick planks and put them side by side, and left him for a while hoping he would slide down them, but when I got back he was still there. Finally, I held a fish in front of his nose and edged it forward slowly, then he moved, placing his flippers onto the planks; he was still not sure whether they were safe or not, but eventually he edged onto them and slowly but surely made his way down. He never attempted to get up on the rockery again.

Having heard how intelligent the grey seals were, I thought I would try to teach Simon a few tricks. I didn't want him to do anything he did not already do but I wanted to see if he would do these things, such as twisting in the water, nosing the ball from one end of the pool to the other and splashing the water with his flipper when he wanted more fish, at my suggestion. So, when it was feeding time I used the word *twist*, gesturing with my hand to show him what I meant. At first, he splashed, then suddenly he twisted. I threw in a fish and tried again. Once more when I said *twist*, and used my hand giving a circular motion, he twisted.

Next I threw the ball to the other end of the pool and used the word *fetch* pointing with my finger. He went after the ball all right, nosed it and came back, so I rewarded him. At least he had gone to the ball. Each time I threw the ball he went after it, but only to toss it out of the water. I thought that was enough for one day, but not Simon, he first twisted, then he waved his flipper in the air, as if trying to splash the water, and, as a last resort, he went to the ball which was floating and flipped it up in the air. I had no fish left so all I could do was to tap him on the head gently and call him a good boy.

Sally, unfortunately, couldn't take part in any of this; all she did was to sit up in the water on one side of the pool. She did not have a lot to do with me, but Simon saw to it that she was never lonely. Whenever he had finished his play with me, he'd chase Sally round the pool and out she would jump followed by Simon's huge bulk right on top of her. Sometimes they made a noise and their teeth seemed to be biting, but they never hurt each other, and all this was only by way of play. Often they would chase each other around, and usually it ended by one or both of them falling into the water. This provided much amusement for the many visitors who came to the Sanctuary. To explain to them why the seals were there and why the Sanctuary existed, we put up posters telling them how the pups had been washed in and the illnesses they had suffered from. All the same I was asked a lot of questions. 'How can a seal catch pneumonia?' or 'Won't they die out of water?' Many people showed great interest in Sally and Simon and some even sent Christmas cards addressed to them. The amount of pleasure that these seals were giving to the old and young alike surprised me; some people had to be dragged away from the Sanctuary as they wanted to stay there all day. A number of them said how much they would love to have seals in their garden, little realising the work involved.

By September, Simon would, on command, ring the bell, fetch the ball, flipping it into my hand, do the twist, splash the water and smack his tummy. These acts he performed without being rewarded with fish.

Every time he saw me he would tease me in the way a

SALLY – A VICTIM OF THE TORREY CANYON

puppy teases his master, running to and fro, sometimes biting at my trousers. Considering that their new home was small, both Sally and Simon were happy, but I was already planning how to make a much bigger pool out of the two small ones.

At the end of September, another newcomer arrived at the Sanctuary. Creamy white coat, bright eyes and not in bad condition. But to make sure we had it injected with an antibiotic, and then tried it with a bowl of milk to see if it would lap – it wouldn't. I decided to buy a calf feeder and find out whether this would be useful for weaning the babies; I wanted anything that would make the process more natural for the baby itself. The calf feeder consisted of an aluminium container with a large screw-on teat at the base. It had a lid and a handle, also a fixture for hanging it on a wall. We kept the milk in the jug, thinking that if the pup would not suck at the teat, we could still use the old tube method.

Now, we put about a quarter of a pint into the container and stuck the teat into the baby's mouth. At first, it kept moving its head and the teat kept coming out, so I held the teat, put it into the pup's mouth and gave it a squeeze, thus letting out a little milk. It bit on the teat but each time it released the hold I gave another squeeze, while keeping its head up high, at last I heard a gulp – it was swallowing the milk. Finally all the milk had gone. At least it had fed without the tube, but the queer part of it was that after moving the feeding apparatus, the pup suckled at my hand. The suction was very strong and why it did not do this on the teat I do not know.

As it was a sunny day we gave the next feed outside. Simon popped up to see who we had now. I started feeding the pup when Simon came alongside me; first he put his head across my lap to sniff at the baby, then, as I was using both my hands on the feeder, he caught hold of my sleeve and began to pull it away. I held the feeder tight in one hand and stroked him with the other till he calmed down. As soon as I had finished feeding the pup, Simon moved in closer to inspect the new arrival more thoroughly. This time I let him have his way, but I did not wish them to get too well acquainted, as this pup would be ready for the open sea in a few weeks' time and it would not be fair to let them make friends only to be parted.

The feeder had done its job. Weaning time was on us. We decided to do it outside so that there would be no fear of straw getting on to the fish. We used small mackerel and had no difficulty in pushing them down. Gradually the pup began to take the fish out of my hand, so, using Sally's pool, I threw a fish into it hoping he would pick it up. If he did, he would be ready for the sea.

'Winstone', as we had named it, made no attempt to go for the fish, so I lowered the next one down to the water beneath his head, and kept on doing this till finally he took a fish when it was immersed in the water. The following day he was picking them up at will and we made up our minds that after another day like this he could have his freedom and perhaps join his family. He had put on a considerable amount of weight and carrying him to the sea would not be easy.

We decided to go early, about six in the morning, hoping there would be no dogs or people to distract Winstone. It is never pleasant taking a seal back to the beaches, one gets attached to any animal and most of these pups had never known their mother and so had come to feel reassurance in our presence. One is left wondering uncomfortably what happens when they meet up with their own kind. It was only later that we proved that they do meet and join other seals, whether these may be their own family or not.

We carried Winstone down to the water's edge and gave him a kiss and a word of good luck. It was sad: that great big ocean in front of us and the little pup which we were leaving alone to fend for himself. However, it would have been wrong to have kept him, Winstone had not been sick, just orphaned. And all we had done was to prepare him for the life he was meant to live.

We put him carefully on the sands and smacked his bottom gently. He made his way into the water, sometimes he gave us a side glance, then he dived under the water and was gone. We watched and glimpsed a little head out in deep water. He made his way around the point and that was the last we saw of Winstone.

CHAPTER FIVE

Intruders

SIMON and Sally were both eating well. Now that Winstone had gone I thought I could spend more time with them but this was not to be, for we soon had another two arrivals. Both were only a few days old and both were males. We called them 'Flipper' and 'Moses' – Moses because we found the baby covered in seaweed.

We divided the shed into two, and put one in each compartment; neither would lap or suckle at the teat, so out came the tube again, this time twice the quantity of milk to be warmed and mixed. By now we found force feeding was fairly easy. Sometimes a pup would play up, but neither Flipper nor Moses caused us too much trouble. We gave four feeds a day. But the pups did not put on weight as they would have had they been suckled by their mothers. However, after losing our first pup by overdoing the fat content of its diet, we had no intention of letting this happen again. So long as the pups kept healthy and gained a little weight we felt it was satisfactory, particularly as we usually weaned them fairly early and they did not have to battle against the sea. In their natural environment they would have had to do just that and would have used up their extra fat while learning to feed themselves.

We had snow that winter, only a few inches, but it was bitter cold. Simon and Sally did not seem to mind it, and Simon dug his nose into the snow and flipped it into the air as he moved along. He would start sliding and, not being able to stop himself, would end up in the pool. This was great fun for him so he repeated it several times over.

Having four seals kept us busy, but we enjoyed every minute of it. Very often I would be covered in muck or milk and people who came to the Sanctuary did not have to ask me if I were the keeper; for one thing they could smell me. Seals have a smell of their own; the babies usually give off a scent of ammonia, which is very noticeable after passing their motion and also when they bite one's clothes their saliva, which has a special odour, gets all over one's sleeves.

Flipper and Moses had settled in, took their milk and then enjoyed a good sleep; their little heads would pop up when Simon barked at Sally. The two new pups brought many people to the Sanctuary, who each day enquired how the babies were getting on.

While they have their creamy white coats, seal pups look quite plump, but when they moult and the grey fur shows, they look much thinner and when in the water look smaller still. I used Sally's pool for Flipper and Moses' first swim, which was fun for them and also cleaned them. As they could not get out on their own, I'd grab hold of their front flippers and give a heave till they slid up. But after a few pulls they managed it for themselves.

Weaning was very easy with Flipper, but with Moses it was much more difficult. We could force feed him, but he would not take fish on his own. Already Flipper was taking fish in the water, so he'd soon be ready for returning to the sea.

That night I locked up, shouted goodnight to all of

them, and went to bed. The following morning I put their fish in the bucket and went over to the Sanctuary. The gate was wide open, Sally and Simon were in the pool, but there was no sign of Flipper and Moses. The lock had been forced open and the two babies were missing. I made a thorough search around the shed, then around the bungalow, but found no sign of them.

I ran in to tell Mary; together we made another search. We went all round the car park behind the bungalow, along the cliff road and finally down the slipway to the beach. There was a track leading down the beach to the sea, we followed it but saw nothing. We did not know whether Flipper or Moses had made the track and we couldn't understand why there was only one track. Had the vandals taken the other seal away? We searched all round the beach, then we went up to the boat pen and looked under all the boats, there was no sign of any track or of a pup. Then I went up to a small building in which we kept a winch for pulling the boats up the beach. At first I could not see a thing, then I heard a faint movement. I went in, looked behind some boxes in the corner and there was Moses. There was blood all round his head and a cut on his body and some on his flippers. He must have been frightened to death and at first he snarled at me.

I kept talking to him and when he realised who I was I was able to pick him up and carry him back to the Sanctuary. On checking his injuries I found that his cuts were not too bad, but whatever had happened during the early hours of that morning had shaken the poor pup very badly.

After settling Moses, we rushed back down to the beach to look for Flipper. We did not feel too bad about him for he had been weaned and should now be able to fend for himself, but we were worried in case he too had been injured. We walked along the water's edge for what seemed hours, then we decided to go on top of the cliff, where we would have a good view over quite a large area. As we were walking we kept on shouting 'Flipper', knowing only too well that the roar of the sea drowned our voices. We felt mad with the world: what sort of person would do such a thing and what satisfaction could they get out of it? A further search was fruitless, but some friends of ours kept watch along the beach in case Flipper might be in difficulty.

The following morning we had another search. At first there was no sign of the pup; then we saw a little head pop up in the water about thirty yards out to sea. We shouted 'Flipper' as loud as we could. He raised himself in the water, but whether or not he heard us I do not know.

We stayed for about an hour, while the pup swam along parallel to the beach. As it was lunch time we then went home, but from our windows we were able to look down on the sea and beach. Just as we had finished our lunch, I looked and saw Flipper roll out of a wave onto the beach. I ran down, but before I got down to the beach he was back in the water.

It looked as if he might be all right though not yet quite settled in his new home. Only one other time did he come on to the beach and again it was only for a few seconds. Often during that summer he swam in the bay and played with the lads on their Malibu or surf-boards. At least it was nice to know that he had made it safely, but that was no thanks to the vandals.

A week later we put Moses back to the sea, but we

never found out if he met up with Flipper, or whether he went his own way and sought his pleasures further down the coastline.

After this encounter we double-locked the gate to the Sanctuary and had no further break-ins.

The following Tuesday evening about five, we had a telephone call telling us of a seal washed in, and badly injured. Darkness was coming down, the winds were blowing gale force and there was heavy rain. It was not too pleasant having to leave a nice warm fire, but we didn't really mind. In any case the poor little thing must be suffering a lot more than we would have to suffer just getting wet and cold.

I started the car, and we gathered all our gear together: Wellingtons, thick coats, scarves, gloves and a torch that showed no more light than a match would. We had nearly thirty miles to go so there was no time to waste, particularly as we couldn't drive very fast since the heavy rain made it difficult to see and the roads were slippery. First, we made for the house of the people who had telephoned to us. As it was so rough and wet we could not ask them to accompany us to the spot where they had seen the seal. But they gave us precise directions, and we started on our trek across the beach. Because we were in a hurry I kept forgetting about Mary and as the light from the torch was very poor, she was left far behind and began shouting at the top of her voice, calling out that she could not see where she was. I had to go back to collect her and then keep shining the torch in front of her as we tried to make our way to our destination.

Because I was shining the torch behind me to help Mary I fell over a rock and went sprawling into a pool of water but, looking up at Mary, I saw that I couldn't be any wetter than she was. Water was dripping all down her face, her trousers were sopping; we looked like a pair of drowned rats. What had we got ourselves into, out on a night like this fetching a sick animal? A few years ago we would never have dreamed that such things could happen to us.

We had one or two further stumbles before we reached the place where the pup was said to be. With the wind blowing into our faces and the torch only giving a glimmer of light, it was like looking for a needle in a haystack. We listened for any noise or movement; suddenly we heard a sneeze just in front of us behind a rock. We edged forward and could just see the seal turning towards us, ready to protect itself against any menace that might be approaching. As we got closer, we could see it was very thin. It had lost its baby coat and had a nasty gash down its back. Obviously here was another pup that had not learned the art of catching fish for itself. When left on its own, it had lived on the fat its mother had provided it with and had then gradually become weak from starvation, also it had been pounded on the rocks and been badly injured. I examined it, and decided it must be got home as quickly as possible, if we were to save its life.

I did not think twice about its biting me and grabbed hold of it quickly, but carefully, so as not to cause it any pain from its cut. I got both arms around the pup's body; Mary shone what little light there was left in the torch and we started back for the car. How I managed to keep going without having to put the pup down on the sands, I don't know. It seemed to get heavier every yard I went, till I was gasping for breath and water was running down my face into my mouth. I was hot and cold both at the same time. It was a relief when we reached the car, but I had no strength left to lift the seal into it. Mary came to my help and between us we got the pup on to the seat, and made it comfortable. Then I had to wait ten minutes to recover from my cold shivery feeling, and also to get my breath back. We threw our wet jackets into the boot but our trousers were drenched and we had a very unpleasant journey.

Before leaving, we notified the people that we had found the pup and then drove home as quickly as possible.

On arrival, we carried the seal into the shed, put on the infra-red lamp to give a little warmth and then we dried ourselves off. Once changed and warmed through we made a check on the pup. The cut was a bad one, but seals' wounds usually heal fairly quickly. The main thing was to stop any infection. We had it injected and obtained powder to rub into the cut to dry and treat the wound. Unfortunately, in spite of all our efforts, it died four days later.

CHAPTER SIX

A Double Tragedy

AT feeding time, there was never any fighting over the fish, Simon and Sally waited patiently for their own share, Simon of course doing his usual tricks. The way they had taken to each other offered good prospects for breeding later on, and we were looking forward to this.

During the summer we had more trouble from people throwing rubbish into the pool: polythene bags, ice cream sticks, dirty old corks and rubber. Each day I had to collect rubbish from the pool and its surroundings although there were many signs asking people not to feed the seals or throw anything into the pool.

I put up more netting to try to stop them, but still they found a way. Even though I was busy in my shop, I made a point of having a peep into the Sanctuary every few hours to check how the visitors were behaving. It had become a great attraction and seemed to give a lot of pleasure to old and young alike. Many of them had never seen a seal before, and few had been so close to one. Simon would come right up to the netting, he loved human beings, but Sally preferred the safety of the pool.

Sometimes there were fifty or more people in the Sanctuary but if I went amongst them and my head showed up, Simon would be out of the water in a jiffy; this proves that seals can recognise one by sight as well as by sound.

The summer season visitors made it difficult for me to

clean the pools. I had to do it after midnight when the business was closed.

The hose-pipe I had fixed up for the seals often caused laughter among the holidaymakers. They'd be enjoying watching the seals play when suddenly Simon would catch hold of the end of the hose-pipe and squirt water over them.

I had been thinking of a way to make one large pool out of the two small ones. When my shop was empty, I drew rough sketches of what might be possible. I had four ship's wheels and I planned to put them into a wall of concrete blocks faced up with stone. Finally, I telephoned to one of my suppliers of concrete slabs and arranged for him to make a hundred white and red two foot square slabs. They would be ready, and hardened off, by the time I needed them.

I also planned to take down my wooden garage and build one of concrete blocks with a room at the end as a sick-bay for seals. I also wanted another sick-room inside the Sanctuary; this would be used for hardening the pups off after being in the heated room attached to the garage. When all this had been done I should be able to cope with quite a lot of babies if several arrived at once, as sometimes happened.

At the end of September I put my plan into operation. I started to dig out the centre piece between the two pools, then, putting up netting close to the edge of the pool, I emptied the top one; after this, I was able to knock through which gave me about sixteen feet to the edge of the pools Simon and Sally were in. So, with their existing pool I could make a pool about twenty-four feet long by twelve feet wide, not extra large, but the largest I could organise at the moment.

When all the earth and rubble were removed, I put in a thick concrete base and then started to build the walls. My plan was to get Simon and Sally over to the part I had built and put netting across to keep them away from the new section I still had to make. The seals would come to no harm if they had to remain on land for a day or two.

When my work was done, the pool was filled and out came Sally with Simon chasing her. The slabs were smooth so they went slithering along them and I think they were proud of their new home.

Our first new pup of the winter came in October, and between that date and December six were washed in. One was in very bad condition and died. The others were successfully weaned and put back to the sea. We were lucky that they were not seriously injured and were able to be weaned at an early age so that they returned to the sea before they had become too attached to us.

Now that the pool was much longer and wider, Simon had a lot more room to show off in; in the middle I had placed a pillar eighteen inches square with a water pipe built into the centre. On this I put a spray; Simon loved it and would leap into the air trying to catch the water, after which he would roll beneath the spray as though he were taking a shower bath.

I had a few lifebelts in the house so I dropped one into the water, another I hung up on to a bar, the belt just resting on the top of the water. First Simon popped his head up through the lifebelt, then he put his flipper over the sides of the belt, using it like a child would in the sea. After that he would try and get on top of the belt, usually falling off at first, then, when his whole body was on, he'd roll on to his back and use it as a float; moving his rear flippers slowly he would travel up and down the pool as if in a boat.

When he got bored with this performance he would swim down to the other lifebelt, put his head and flippers through it and support his whole body in it; it acted just like a see-saw balanced in the middle; on this he would go to sleep. When Simon didn't use the belt, Sally would get inside it.

In May of that year, 1968, Simon had another attack of lung trouble; he looked really rough. I emptied the pool and put a large dose of antibiotic in a fish, but he wouldn't eat it. I rang my vet and asked him to come quickly and give Simon an injection, for this was the only other way of treating his complaint.

Again I had to hurt Simon's pride by holding him tight while he was being injected. Although I could do anything with him when no one else was in the pool, as soon as the vet appeared he would snap at anyone. After a struggle, we managed to inject him, then he was left to rest and Sally came up to his side as if to comfort him. A few days later Simon seemed to be himself again and I filled the pool.

But by the first week in June he didn't look well. I treated him with antibiotics; they had no effect. I watched him closely during the next few days, in fact I couldn't settle to work in my shop where people came in constantly to tell me how poorly Simon was looking.

One morning Simon wouldn't eat. I wasn't too worried about this as sometimes seals have a fasting period, but the trouble was that if he didn't eat I could not give him his medicine. About mid-day I went out to see him, he was gasping for breath and looked really sorry for himself. Having been with seals for so long

Sally II meets new pup

Simon II asks her to come into the pool

The sea-lions Kim and Judy

Baby seals
hardening off in
their new homes

I could now tell when they were off colour and when their condition was serious, and I knew that Simon was very ill indeed.

I rang the vet; he came rushing out, but by the time he arrived Simon was in the water cuddling Sally gently. The vet was inclined to think that I had brought him out for nothing. He said Simon seemed all right and left.

A little later I went back to the pool. Simon came to the side; he held his nose slightly out of the water and curling his body up squeezed his neck making it twice its normal size.

I called to him, but he paid no attention. Sally came over and sniffed him, but he took no notice. Then, after five minutes, he suddenly swam around the pool, returned to the same place and started to gasp for breath. He went under water, but in a few seconds was back up again, this time he was gasping still harder.

I held his head above water. He looked pleadingly at me as though trying to tell me something I couldn't understand. I spoke to him gently thinking this was only another attack, such as he had previously had and recovered from.

After a few minutes I released his head, but again he gasped and this time he went into a frenzy, then suddenly he seemed to be drowning. I quickly turned the stopcock to empty the pool. As the water slowly went down, Simon gave a sudden leap up into the water and made a dive back, which gave me a fright. I realised that he couldn't breathe, so I jumped into the pool – clothes and all – and held his head above water, but he didn't stir. He weighed about five hundredweight so I couldn't lift him. I waited until all the water was out of the pool – it only took a few minutes to empty – but it seemed hours to me. Then I shook Simon and spoke to him, but he had no reaction. My first thought then was that he was dead. But that couldn't be. I gave him artificial respiration, with no result. I shouted to a visitor asking him to ring my vet urgently and I told him what to say. But soon I realised that Simon had left us. He had been slowly dying for the last few hours, but he could not tell me. He had given Sally a cuddle, perhaps he knew that he was leaving her. Sally being practically blind, was so dependent on him, he was her protector; had he given her a last expression of affection to console her for what was to follow?

Simon was lying on his back. Sally came up to us and crawled up on to his tummy and scratched his body with her flippers. She pushed at him with her nose, scratching at the same time. As she was doing this I suddenly noticed tears falling from her eyes, not the normal watering that seals sometimes have, but real tears. (I must admit I too had tears in my eyes.) We had both lost a part of ourselves, the affection Simon had shown us during the six years he had been with us will never be forgotten; he had become part of our family.

Except for the occasional illness, he had lived a happy life and had given happiness to people from all over the country. We shall always remember Simon.

Sally kept edging up to his head. I'm sure she knew he was dead. She lay motionless by him, tears still coming from her eyes. Up to now I had never been able to fuss Sally, now I put my hand gently on her back and she didn't stir, so I stroked her, gradually moving my hand up to her head; under normal circumstances I wouldn't have dared attempt this. I think both of us must have been in a state of shock. I stroked her head as one would a dog's and gently she lifted it and put it across my arm. I couldn't believe it. She rested her head there crying like a baby.

I thought that Sally's grief must be much deeper than mine. Her blindness had made her nervous, but at least when Simon was there she was protected and comforted.

The vet arrived. He examined Simon to make sure that he was dead. He said that after seeing him earlier that day cuddling Sally he couldn't believe it and suggested a post mortem. Although we had previously carried out occasional post mortems on pups, I dreaded it. But the vet said that as Simon's health had been bad from the start, a sudden death was to be expected at some stage and now, by examining his lungs something might be learned to help future pups suffering from similar conditions. If knowledge could be gained by a post mortem, then I must agree.

We decided it could be done in the shed at the side of the pool. Sally was still lying on Simon's body so we had to move her in order to get him out. By holding Simon's head and back flippers we tried to ease his body from under her, but she gripped him tightly and wasn't going to let him be taken away. Finally, as we slid the body carefully along the bottom of the pool, Sally became very upset and tried to bite the vet's hand.

We then fetched a large plastic sheet and rolled it underneath Simon and asked two strong men to give us a lift which they did willingly. As we tried to lift the body Sally hung on as hard as she could. It was pitiful to watch her, but Simon's corpse had in any case to be removed.

All this proves that animals have as deep feelings as we do. They love, feel and weep as any person would.

We carried Simon into the shed, closed the door and the vet prepared for the post mortem. When we saw his lungs, we realised that nothing could have saved him. Over a period of years they had deteriorated, and one had collapsed. At least, he had never suffered any pain. I arranged with a local farmer to fetch the body and have it buried in a friend's field nearby. When the tractor came to take it away people gathered around asking questions, but I was unable to answer them.

When I went back into the pool, Sally was lying there motionless. I spoke to her softly trying to comfort her. She let me stroke her. All this had taken an hour and a half and Mary knew nothing of what had happened. I smoked a cigarette and drank a cup of tea to steady me, then I went to the restaurant. Mary was in the kitchen; she turned round. I expect my face looked a sight as she and the waitress asked if I were all right. 'Simon's dead,' I said. There was silence, which was finally broken by Mary asking a few questions: when, how, why?

I had a cup of tea and went back down to the shop only to be further upset many times by visitors who knew Simon and asked how he was. In the end I wrote out a statement saying that Simon had died that day and I posted it up in the Sanctuary. Hundreds of people came into the shop and expressed their sympathy.

The next few days were very trying; Sally wouldn't eat and though she accepted all the fuss I made of her, she showed no interest whatsoever. I had her injected for shock and gave her a booster, but still she wouldn't eat. Last thing at night I would go and talk to her, but she just stared into space.

A week after Simon's death, Sally too died. She had pined herself to death. A post mortem showed a healthy body, but heartbreak has no physical signs. We placed her body next to Simon's and can only hope that in spirit they are together again.

It was a terrible shock to us to lose our two dear seals in one week but nothing could have saved them. Many seals will no doubt come my way, but never again one like Simon, of that I am sure.

CHAPTER SEVEN

Sea-Lions in the Sanctuary

IT was June and thousands of people came to visit the Sanctuary, only to find it empty. But it wasn't long before two sea-lions, suffering from worm in the lungs and intestines arrived; they came from a zoo. It seemed that, by now, people had come to think of me as someone who was always ready to care for sick or injured animals. After handling grey seals they seemed very queer to us. They were so lively and the speed at which they could move was something to which we were not accustomed. A sea-lion walks on its front and back flippers, moving in leaps and bounds; when walking slowly it has a sort of wobble, like a woman walking in a very tight skirt. They also differ in many other ways from the Atlantic grey seal.

The sea-lion is called the eared seal, having ear lobes about an inch and a half long, whereas the grey seal has only two small openings hardly noticeable unless they are listening to something, when two small horns project out of the orifices.

The sea-lion's front flippers are long, black and rubbery and have no gripping parts; they are used mainly for swimming and, of course, for walking on. It is they which give the sea-lion a sweeping effect and ensure its speed in the water. The back flippers, which can be tucked underneath the body when on land, are used as rudders in the sea. Their flippers are not at all like those of the grey seals which are short, thick, hand-like flippers with long thick nails in front, it is with these 'gripping hands' that seals climb rocks and pull their great bulk out of the water; the back flippers which they use for propulsion in the sea have no use on land.

Sea-lions look more streamlined, partly because they have a smaller head. The grey seal has a thick body which tapers to a point at the back flippers, its head is much broader than that of the sea-lion, indeed it is often called 'Horse Head'. Because the sea-lion has a graceful appearance and movement it is very popular in circuses, and they are trained to do many tricks.

We named our sea-lions Judy and Kim. They found the pool empty of water. We had our reasons for this; they had come in large wire crates, so now we lowered them down into the pool and opened the doors. Out came Judy, giving a most alarming and unusual bark. She wasn't very big, but as fast as lightning. I jumped out of the pool, to give her time to get used to her new surroundings. I then gave her a few fish, surprisingly, she took them gently out of my hand. I moved the empty crate out, and opened Kim's door. He was much more frightening than Judy and flew out giving a loud, deep bark. At this I rushed out of the pool, but, to my amazement, so did he! I didn't realise sea-lions were so agile. Judy didn't find it quite so easy, but after a little straining, she too was out. I didn't know which way to turn, if they had been grey seals I would not have been frightened, but these beasts could move faster than I could.

Kim climbed up my rockery and before I knew what he was at, he was on top of my garage, which, at the back, was level with the car park. Another second and he was running around the cars. I grabbed his cage and ran after him. Finally some visitors helped me to drive him into his cage. This meant I must at once put up netting to keep the two seals in safety.

It took two days to make the whole Sanctuary secure; meanwhile I set up boards high enough to stop them from climbing out.

I filled the pool and watched the sea-lions' graceful action in water and admired the ease with which they flew out of the pool. When they were ashore they slid along the smooth slabs; they enjoyed this so much that they soon started taking short runs, falling on their tummy and sliding along the side of the pool from one end to the other.

I had an old mirror, which I fixed on to the wall and they would slide up to it, fighting for a good position from which to admire themselves, after which they would walk backwards into the pool. I suppose they were fascinated by seeing another sea-lion in the mirror backing away from them.

Scratching was another of their entertainments; they would sit on their bottoms, lift one back flipper and scratch their chins. They were too nervous to allow me to stroke them, but they never attempted to bite me, though they would come roaring past and knock me over if I were not careful.

I made a strong wooden platform for them to sleep on, but no, they preferred to sleep in their cages which I had placed inside the shed.

Judy and Kim were given treatment once a week because they were covered with spots, these were caused by the migration of a worm around the bodies. They also coughed and brought up worms from their lungs. One day I found a tape worm three feet long in the pool.

When I first saw it I thought that someone had thrown a shoelace in.

Judy seemed to be the boss, she was very mischievous; Kim liked his afternoon nap in the shed, but Judy would soon turn him out in spite of his grunts of displeasure at having his sleep disturbed.

The barks of the two sea-lions were worse than their bites. They often made a lot of noise even when playing, and looked as though they were fighting, but this was their way of enjoying themselves.

The main thing now was to keep down the worms for if they penetrated the lungs deeply, then the sea-lions would certainly die.

CHAPTER EIGHT

Simon II and Sally II

It was again September and, if the weather was rough, we could expect some pups to come in soon.

The first came on the 2nd of October, it was a pup about a week old. As the business was closed we had all the time we needed to care for it.

We gave it milk feeds four times a day for about a week, by which time a second pup had arrived.

Often we imagine that we are going to have an easy winter, but in fact, we usually end up with roughly the same number of pups; the ages, of course, vary from a day old to two or three weeks but nearly all of them have not yet been weaned.

Baby seals, while they still have their creamy white coats, look alike; it is when they lose these that one is able to tell them apart even from a distance. Each one then has its own characteristic appearance. But even after this, local people still ask which is which, and to them they look the same, though when you have been caring for them, you feel like a person with ten children, who, even if they look alike to strangers, present no problem of identification to their parents.

These two pups were successfully weaned on to fish and returned to sea, as were two others that came in a little later, but one that arrived during November stayed with us. We called him Simon II, because he had the same temperament, and looked very much like our old

Simon; he even had the same complaint, pneumonia, which was going to need long term treatment. We gave him antibiotics, and kept him indoors for quite a long period. Weaning him on to fish proved no problem.

It was January when he was first introduced to the pool and also to a meeting with Judy and Kim. I didn't know what would happen when we put a grey seal in with the sea-lions, so I was prepared for any emergency.

Almost immediately Simon II and Judy's noses came together, then he made a fast getaway, but Judy did two circles around him before he reached the end of the pool. Kim took no notice of him.

Judy's speed was terrific, so at feeding times I had to throw her fish up to the far end of the pool, then quickly throw Simon's just beside me, or she would get the lot. Kim usually took his out of my hand.

In March of that year, a woman from a nearby resort drove over to tell us that there was a badly injured seal on their beach. I followed her back in my car; she had about six children with her, and they were all much excited.

I expected the seal to be either an adult or about five to six months old, as I had never found a young pup at this time of year. As the tide was out, we had a long walk over the beach; when we finally got to the place where the seal had been, I could not see a sign of it so I walked up to the base of the cliff. There, in between some rocks, I saw a small pup, about three weeks old. It was thin and, looking closely at it, I noticed that its neck was torn open, either someone had put a rope around it, or it had been caught in a fishing line – it looked really bad. As I went to pick it up it started to move away so I let it stop of its own accord, then I put one arm under its chin and the other under its tummy. I tried to be as careful as possible as I didn't wish to cause any further damage to its neck.

I saw that it was a female, and was suffering from shock. I had a long way to carry her along the beach, and I thought 'this is where a jeep ambulance would be useful', for with it treatment could have been given on the spot and warmth and comfort provided at once.

I had to rest at intervals, putting the seal down on the sands while I did so. The children kept asking if she would die; I assured them that she would have the best possible care and that I thought she would get well.

When we reached the car, I put her on the seat, thanked the children and the woman who had come with us and told them they could visit the Sanctuary at any time to see her. Then I got home as quickly as I could, made a bed of straw, switched on the infra-red lamp and put it in a safe position where the seal couldn't get at it. I now had a good look at the pup's neck, and then rang my vet and gave him all the details of the case. A little later he arrived, checked her over and gave her an injection.

That night we had no sleep as the pup's breathing had worsened and it looked as if we might lose her. We didn't put her on to milk, but weaned her straight on to fish: small quantities every two or three hours.

Next day, the vet came again and gave the pup a thorough examination which showed that she was in a very bad condition. Her lungs were severely congested, indeed, she was now gasping through her mouth for air. Her two gashes were deep and infected, they were close together and had jagged edges, so the vet said he must treat the injuries as an open wound for they were too wide to stitch up. The cuts were thoroughly cleaned and sprayed with antiseptic and every few hours I dabbed gently at them with antiseptic powder and cotton wool, getting the powder well down into the wound. The pup was very good while I treated her neck, as if she knew that I was trying to help her. Many more sleepless nights followed that first one.

At one time her breathing was so bad, and her nose so blocked up that we decided to use Vick to loosen and bring up the mucus. I placed it regularly on her nose and it proved successful. Although she had let me treat the wound, I had to use a stick to put the Vick on and she snapped when I tried to stroke her tummy.

Sally II, as we decided to call her, was in for a long spell of intensive care. Gradually the wound dried up and began to heal; her breathing remained bad, but the Vick made it possible for her to breathe at times through her nose.

Sally must have been just over three weeks old when I picked her up for she had recently lost her puppy coat.

Weaning her onto fish was awkward, as we didn't want to hurt her while holding her in order to force the fish down. Normally, pups have to be held quite firmly while doing this, but in Sally's case we had to be very gentle. However, each day feeding became a little easier and we thought her condition must have improved as she snapped out after putting down her food. This is a normal thing for a healthy pup to do; affection is not gained quickly, trust has to be built up on each side and this takes time.

After five weeks I moved Sally to another pen; her breathing was slightly easier but she was still passing mucus from her nose. When she heard the other seals splashing in the pool, she used to climb the netting and obviously wanted to see what was going on. On the way to their sleeping pen Judy and Kim had to pass the netting and that was how she first met them. I felt that Sally II might be going to be yet another Simon. For one thing, I knew she would never be able to be returned to the sea, her lungs were sure to remain weak just as his had.

After hardening her off for a few weeks, I introduced her to the pool. She slithered into the water, then there was a commotion, flippers were flying everywhere. She jumped out at my feet and let me stroke her, after which she went back into the water. Simon II chased her round the pool, sniffing at her back as they moved around; Judy also joined in, but not Kim, he went back to bed, as if to say 'not another!'

I kept close watch on Sally, in case one of the seals turned on her, but in fact she was accepted as if she belonged among them. Simon was certainly excited and I began to think it meant love at first sight; Judy, perhaps disapproving, just kept pecking at her. I smiled at myself as I watched Simon chasing Sally around the pool and she, popping her head up occasionally to look at me with her big bright eyes, plainly wondering how she could throw off this big fat hulk of a seal. I was very pleased to see her playing as though she had never been ill. This was one of the moments that made me feel on top of the world and convinced me that the job of rescuing seals can be rewarding as well as, at times, disheartening.

CHAPTER NINE

The Suffering that People can cause

Now it was time to get my business going, for Whitsun starts the season and we have many holidaymakers from then until September. It was during the next few weeks that the vandals started up again. First, some ornaments were stolen, then things were thrown into the pool; children were allowed to paddle in the fish pond and my outside wall was kicked down by people climbing over it.

By the time August came, I was preparing to stop the public from entering the Sanctuary and for one brief moment I was nearly ready to stop having one. Sally was hit on the head by a brick, one of several which had been thrown from the car park behind the canopy into the pool, and Simon had swallowed a ball, which had been thrown into the pool by a child whose parents were present at the time. (I didn't see this myself, but a visitor came straight down to the shop to inform me.)

Why do people do these things? I have signs telling them not to throw anything into the pool and also telling them of previous damage caused by such actions.

I rushed up to the pool and first looked at Sally; she was holding her head above water, her eyes bulging. Normally, as I passed the netting surrounding the pool, she would jump out, but now she seemed to be staring into space. There was a mark on the top of her head, but no blood. The first thing I suspected was concussion.

Next I looked at Simon; he seemed all right, and I supposed that to him swallowing a ball was like swallowing a fish. I checked with the visitors that they had actually seen him swallow the ball, they all confirmed that he had.

I emptied the pool so that I could check Sally over more thoroughly; there was no cut, but there was a depression in her skull. I pressed lightly on it to see if this caused her any pain; it was difficult to judge whether it did, more still to tell what damage had been done. I went back to the shop, telephoned to my vet and told him that neither seal seemed to be in any pain, but that Sally probably had concussion and that Simon had swallowed a ball. The exact size of the ball was not known, my informants said it was a little larger than a golf ball. What I was worried about now was whether the ball would block his stomach as the straw had done to Sammy. We discussed what could be done to help Sally; if brain damage had occurred then we were in serious trouble, for an operation would have meant certain death.

We decided first to dose Simon with liquid paraffin; this would give lubrication and perhaps help the ball to pass along the intestines. So far as Sally was concerned, we must wait to see if any further symptoms developed, if they did they could help us to diagnose her injury; she might only be stunned and, if so, would recover quickly.

I went back to the pool and fussed Sally, but she didn't seem to know I was there. At that moment, if I could have laid my hands on the person responsible for her state, I'm afraid I would have taken the law into my own

Oiled guillemots

Blacky's eyes and body showing burn marks

Playtime never ends for seals . . .

... or badgers

hands and who knows what the outcome would have been. A friendly neighbour volunteered to keep watch on both the seals while I went back to the shop, but every half hour I popped out to see how they were. I was anxious about the ball; if Simon were going to pass it how long would that take? Luckily he was still eating so I was able to put liquid paraffin into his fish and, if he didn't eat, he was so fat that if the ball blocked the stomach, he could live quite a while on his own fat. Sally ate very little, but I wasn't too worried about that; she too had had a good appetite and was well able to starve for a few days without its having any ill effects.

Before I went to bed, I spent some time watching them. I might just as well not have gone to bed, for Mary and I stayed awake and I was up early checking again. Simon looked up as I entered the pool, which was still empty, making it easy for me to check the motion he passed and also rest Sally without having to distress her by carrying her into isolation. In a case such as this one, company would do wonders especially as Sally was probably more sick in mind than in body.

She lay motionless; suspecting the worst I jumped in quickly, afraid to touch her in case she were dead. I stroked her gently, her body was warm; then she lifted her head and laid it down again as if she hadn't seen me, no doubt she didn't see me. I spoke to her; Sally's ears remained closed; I wondered whether she could hear me; I didn't think she could. She seemed to be blind and deaf too.

I felt sick. What had they done to the poor little thing? As if she hadn't gone through enough already. Tears came to my eyes at the thought of the stupidity of the people who could hurt any animal in such a way, and I realised, with a shock, that this could have happened to my dog or even to my daughter if irresponsible people threw bricks. Now it was up to me to make the Sanctuary safe from any vandals without spoiling the pleasures of the many people who were taking an interest in the seals. I had received letters from a school in Holland whose children had sent a small donation collected by selling old toys and sweets (their teacher comes over each year to take photographs). Canada was another part of the world from which I had had letters, many had come at the time of the culling of the pups in the Gulf of St Lawrence. From Malawi, too, I had had encouraging support.

It was fine that people of different nations showed an interest in the welfare of animals and it made us feel good to receive these letters of appreciation for the work we were trying to do: certainly, I must keep the Sanctuary going.

That day brought no change; Simon didn't seem to suffer any ill effects, but Sally showed no interest in anything that went on. I posted a notice explaining what had happened to the seals.

Forty-eight hours went by and Simon still hadn't passed the ball. The following afternoon, after seventy hours, I was relieved to see it appear; it was solid rubber with ragged edges and was the size of a golf ball. Had it been any bigger I don't think Simon would be alive today.

Now we had Sally to hope for. I thought I'd like to see if she had any reaction if the pool were filled, so I filled it that night to Simon's great delight. Kim and Judy too, were pleased.

Simon at once started teasing Sally, but he got no

response; she sat up in the pool staring into space, then she suddenly gave a yell and spun round like a top. This amused the spectators, who thought it was an act; when I told them what had happened to her their reaction was different. I shouted to Sally but she did not respond. When Simon again went near her she flipped him and gave a sudden dive to the other end of the pool. She now ate a little but only if I put the fish into her mouth; if it dropped out she left it, she didn't seem to see it. However, she was at least getting sufficient food to keep her going. There was nothing we could do for her surgically, so love and affection, and the passing of time, would offer her only hope of a cure.

Judy, Kim and Simon did their best to entertain her, but nothing seemed to have any effect on her. Friends kept watch whilst I was busy; they told me how many times she did her spinning act. At feeding time she took a little fish, but did not show much interest in it. I kept on telling Simon to show her some affection, and he must have sensed what I meant, as he slowly approached her, gently sniffing her neck and then lay on his back, brushing up against her. This state of affairs went on for a few weeks, after this Sally gradually came to the side of the pool and resting on her back, let me stroke her stomach. She now ate much better and started moving around the pool a bit. One evening when I closed the shop, I went in to inspect her, and found that Simon was cuddling her, and that she seemed to be enjoying herself. I crept quietly away. This, I thought, could be the turning point.

Next morning she ate like her old self, even fighting Simon for the fish. I was very pleased. She had been through a rough time from her birth onwards, and I was determined that no further harm should come to her. I set up a canopy over part of the pool which would prevent stones from being thrown in and also provided a shelter for the seals; over the other part I placed netting. The seals were now safe, as well as happy.

CHAPTER TEN

A Disastrous Winter

SEPTEMBER 1969 started off in the usual way. When a pup was washed in on our beach a friend woke us up at seven o'clock in the morning, he was carrying a little seal in his arms. It was about two or three days old and remains of the umbilical cord could still be seen; its bright eyes looked up at me, while it rested its head on my friend's forearm. The pup had patches of oil on its creamy white fur; it weighed about twenty-five to thirty pounds which meant it was in good condition as regards weight, but it was beginning to run at the nose showing that congestion of the lungs had developed, which if not treated would lead to pneumonia.

The shed was ready, all I had to do was put down some straw; this took only a few minutes and then the pup was placed on to a warm bed. I fixed up the infra-red lamp and started treatment immediately. The next thing was to inject it with an antibiotic; I rang my vet who came at once. We injected into the fatty part near the hind quarters and further doses were given on the following day in its milk feed. All that was now needed was warmth, regular food and rest.

Four days later a couple from St Ives rang us up to say that they had just visited Hell's Mouth and seen a baby seal in difficulty on the beach. A young fisherman was keeping his eye on it while they were phoning me. The fisherman had told them that the pup was in a terrible state; it looked as though its stomach were hanging out. We asked the couple if, so as to avoid any delay in our finding it, they could stay at the place where we would have to turn off the road.

We put our usual gear into the car and raced away. The twelve miles we had to go didn't take us long. We took the car down the lane as far as we could, then started off on foot.

We had a long walk before reaching the top of the cliff; then I saw a narrow path with only just enough room for us to walk down it in single file. It was a very steep slope indeed with a dangerous drop on the seaward side and we had to be very cautious.

I had a jacket in which I intended to wrap the seal; I put this on my outside arm, using the other to hold on to the grass in case I slipped.

Mary was with me when I started from the car and so were the young couple who had rung us up. I looked back up the slope and saw that they had just reached the cliff's edge. On looking down again I saw the young fisherman by the seal and I noted that the tide was only a few feet away, so I made as much haste as I could with safety.

When I reached the boy, he asked me if I were going to put the pup out of its misery. I examined it; the sea had just reached where it lay so I gently turned it over. I was expecting a frightful sight but all I saw was the umbilical cord hanging out; the lad had evidently mistaken this for the seal's stomach. While I was making further checks a wave came rolling in and drenched me, it also started to drag the pup away on its backwash. I had to be quick now or it would be taken out to sea. I picked it up just in time as another roller came in. In

A DISASTROUS WINTER

fact, I caught the full force of the wave and only managed with some difficulty to hold my feet firm.

While all this was going on, Mary and the others had reached the beach; they feared I was going to be washed out to sea when that last wave hit me.

I looked up the path we had to climb and knew I was in for a rough time. Carrying thirty pounds of seal up a three-in-one slope, where there was only just room for foothold and a drop of a few hundred feet down to the sea, was going to be a little breathtaking. I made the baby as comfortable as I could across my arms and started on the long pull up. Each step I took the seal seemed to get heavier; sometimes its back flippers would touch the gorse on the bank and then it would wriggle to get free. This made things worse for me, as my arms were getting very tired, so I got down on one knee holding tight on to the pup. The cliff looked frightening and I knew that the least movement might send us both tumbling down. My breathing was very difficult and I had to rest every few minutes before I started off on the climb again.

I was happy when I reached the flat top. There was still quite a way to go, but the worst was over, though by now I was completely breathless and when I was well on to the grass, I put the seal down.

Mary said I looked like a ghost and I certainly felt like one; but after a few minutes I was able to make for the car. We put the pup on the back seat. It looked healthy enough so we hoped we would be able to prepare it for the sea. On arriving home, I made a clean bed of straw and settled the baby down on it. Just in case of any infections I called the vet out to inject it and then it was left to rest. Two hours later the pup was dead. We couldn't understand it.

A post mortem was carried out and showed congestion of the lungs and septicaemia. Septicaemia is a form of blood poisoning and was secondary to its other condition; it was the first time I had come across it in seals, but later it became very common and nearly seventy pups were to die of starvation, lung congestion and septicaemia in the months that followed.

My next call was from a man living thirty miles up the coastline; he had found a baby seal only a few days old and wanted to know how to feed it. He wished to do this himself so I explained what he would need to do.

The following day I rang him up to see how he had managed as I knew it wouldn't be easy for him. He told me the pup had died four hours after he had found it. Again the cause of death proved to be septicaemia and again this one had looked a healthy pup.

Further calls came from St Ives stating that three seals had been washed in dead. Then came one from the Lizard saying that a baby seal had been washed in with its eyes destroyed. I arranged to meet the man who had found it, half way to the Lizard so that I could get to my vet more quickly. They had put the seal in a net and it was easy to handle; I had a quick look, the eyes looked very bad, and the seal was very thin. It had already lost its white coat but I do not think it weighed more than fifteen pounds; at this age it should have been around sixty to eighty pounds.

I went straight to the vet as the pup's condition was so serious and it was also suffering from shock. We laid it gently on the table, and while doing so one eyeball ran out on to the table so that eye was completely gone. The other wasn't quite so bad and the vet injected it

A DISASTROUS WINTER

against all likely infections. I rushed it back to the Sanctuary, but the following day it was dead; the post mortem again showed malnutrition, lung congestion and septicaemia. What was happening? We were unable to save these pups. Why were this year's pups different from earlier ones? I began to worry and after a few more phone calls telling me of other baby seals washed in dead and getting a report of adult seals coming ashore at the Lizard with what looked rather like burns and of still others gasping for breath, I decided to call in the Seal Research Unit to see if they had any views as to what might be causing these deaths.

Soon after this, television and the press carried the story. Our telephone began to ring non-stop, our house became something like a newspaper office and we were surrounded by television cameras. Since we were at the time full up with starving pups who needed the most intensive care and we were also being constantly called out to rescue others who had been washed in, we had quite a problem to get through all our tasks and give interviews as well.

Mr Bonner, of the Seal Research Unit, and I decided that we ought to make a survey of as many beaches as we could.

Two journalists from the *Sun* and two from the *Evening Standard* volunteered to help us.

We started on our local beaches and worked our way down the coastline by Chapel Porth, Porthtowan, Portreath and Godrevy from which we had had a report that there were two baby seals on the beach. We contacted the man who had informed us and he gave us directions which we followed.

We had to go by a place where after a steep slope there

was a terrific sheer drop, it was practically vertical and to look down was frightening.

We eased our way along the first part but the final drop was going to be very difficult. I had a short length of rope with me and was lowered down as far as it reached, after that, I made my way as best I could down the last lap.

I could see one baby seal lying between two rocks, the other was in the water, both looked very thin. I could do nothing about the one that was in the sea and just hoped that it would wean itself onto fish before it was too late.

The pup between the rocks was in a very bad condition and had lung congestion. I placed my old jacket round it and made a comfortable hold round its body to enable me to clamber back over the rocks to the base of the cliff. I saw the reporters half way down the rockface waiting for me, then one was lowered so that he could take photographs of the rescue.

My problem was how to get the seal up the sheer part of the cliff. The rope would be of no use and I would need help. I carried the pup as far as I could. Then I asked the photographer to stop taking shots and to hold the seal. First, I wrapped my jacket round its head so that the man should not get bitten, then I explained to him what he had to do and handed him the pup.

I had quite a struggle to reach the first ledge. When I had made it, I dug a good foothold in the shale. Then I reached down to take the pup from the photographer. I stretched as far as I safely could, an inch more and I should have toppled over, but I could not reach the seal. I asked the photographer to try and lift it as high as he could. By now I had been joined by a reporter, he dug in his foothold behind me and held onto the back of my coat to prevent me from slipping. Like this I was able to stretch a little farther and managed to get one hand onto the seal's back flipper. I held on like grim death, for I knew it was now or never. The reporter hung onto my jacket, as hard as he could, the photographer pushed up as high as he could but then he shouted that he was afraid he'd have to let go. The pup was now hanging by its flipper which I was holding, and its weight was getting too much for me.

I called to the photographer to try to put the jacket round its head to prevent it from twisting and snarling. Then I heard a yell, he had been bitten on the thumb. Nevertheless he managed to cover the pup's head and to ease the weight and I heaved it onto the ledge. After this I crawled up the next hundred feet.

Even when we had reached the top of the cliff our troubles were not over for the car was three quarters of a mile away and for most of that distance we had to walk through thick brambles, this made it impossible for me to put the pup down and give myself a rest until we reached a field. Over the last few hundred yards I had to rest many times but I made it.

I had expected the reporters to catch up with me but there was no sign of them and I went back to the top of the cliff to have a look. There I discovered that the photographer was stuck on a ledge, so I crawled down to him, after which we pulled him up slowly.

Finally we all went back to the Sanctuary.

The newspaper men had risked their lives to try to save a seal pup, and one would have a scarred thumb to remind him of his good deed; they also had a big story and photographs to prove its truth. It is sad that the pup, like most of the others we had rescued during this season died of lung congestion, septicaemia and starvation.

Seals still went on coming in on most beaches, some dead, others in a very bad state; one came from St Austell. We had never before had reports of seals washed in there; again this one was dying of starvation.

We rushed it back for treatment. The vet had little hope for it, but we hoped something could be done. Already nearly thirty pups had died and this was four times the normal number of pups washed in at this season.

Scientists came down to investigate; checks were made on seals washed in with burn marks, also on fish that had ulcers. Every possible cause was considered.

Many thousands of sea birds had died in a similar way to these baby seals; the post mortems and tests on the birds had shown that PCB and DDT were present in high quantities. Quite a number of my seal pups died in convulsions. It was pitiful to see them; they had used up all their fat until they were only skin and bone, and no doubt this had left them open to any diseases. Were the seals being poisoned by effluent from some plant? Were the fish being poisoned?

It was easy to blame every sort of pollution. Had the detergents to clean the beaches of the *Torrey Canyon* oil been involved in what had happened and was still happening?

We hoped that the scientists would find the answer; in the meantime our object was to treat the sick seals, but how could we do this without knowing the cause of their condition? The scientists worked hard, but in the end they failed to find any evidence of pollution being involved.

From having seven to ten pups to care for each winter, we were now over the forty mark – and how many more were going to come?

All Cornwall was as worried as we were, for one of our main industries is fishing and we didn't want people panicking about poisoned fish.

We checked on the reports of seals with burns, none were found. Then we decided to hire a boat and again investigate the coastline and the sea close to the cliffs to see how many more babies might be floating around in trouble.

The boat pulled out of harbour at nine thirty in the morning. We had hoped for a good day, but the north-westerly wind blew and we began to rock. Like a fool, I went below where there was a new oil stove belching fumes. The sea tossed us about like a cardboard box and I could hardly hold onto the seat. I soon started to sweat and felt sick, so I went quickly on deck where, after a few whiffs of fresh air, I was all right again.

The pathologist of the Seal Research Unit was with us; we made our first stop at Seal Island. In the summer there are always quite a number of seals basking in the sun on the rocks, and many visitors take trips out to the Island to see them; but now there wasn't a seal in sight. We had a good look and then went farther along the coastline.

We used powerful glasses to check the caves and beaches normally inaccessible to man. We couldn't see any bodies, but suddenly we saw a little head popping up out of the water. That seal at least seemed to be all right – indeed, he was very inquisitive and kept watch on us.

I thought, 'at least one has survived, even though we

have lost nearly a whole generation of pups.' We carried on surveying the cliff line and the water's edge; in all we saw five seals, all young ones, but not one adult was in sight.

We decided to call it a day, the skipper turned the boat around, and we headed home. When we arrived near the harbour we had to wait an hour for the tide to give us sufficient water to make it. We were cold and hungry, but we had satisfied ourselves that no adult seals were in trouble.

I was anxious to get home as we had four pups at the Sanctuary. We always name our seals; the new arrivals were called Flipper, Jenny, Fatima and Blacky.

They were on fish, but Fatima and Blacky still had to be force fed; it was a full time job. The fish was prepared, Sally, Simon, Judy and Kim were fed. Then I concentrated on the babies. Flipper and Jenny were fed next; they took the fish from my hand, but were kept in their pens for the moment as they had a long way to go before they would be back to normal. Fatima's meal came third, and now Mary had to help. I got into the pen, held the seal's head high, forced her mouth open and Mary pushed the fish down. At this stage, the pup was having seven mackerel three times a day; this made up between five and six pounds of fish. Blacky was put in a separate pen, away from the others; he was still a very sick seal with a very bad eye. He had a queer habit of charging at me snarling and then suddenly rolling over. It was undoubtedly a game as he did it a few times before and after each feed, but I couldn't take any chances with him for very often he would tear at my coat – as long as it wasn't my skin I didn't mind.

Blacky was given the same amount of fish as Fatima;

this was a little less than Flipper and Jenny, yet Blacky and Fatima seemed to put on more fat than the two others. Probably this was because they had had a better start in life than the little ones. It wasn't easy to feed Jenny and Flipper as, although I had fed Judy and Sally before them, they would jump out of the pool near the babies' pens and try to take the fish out of my hand; and this would raise a crying snarl from Flipper and Jenny.

After a week, I decided to let Flipper into the pool; I opened the door and out he came following in my footsteps. He sniffed at the water, but that was all, he was more interested in getting a little fuss from me. Finally, I had to give him a push and splash – he had his first swim. With his fur wet, he looked tiny beside the others. They swam up to have a look at the new arrival and all were gentle with him, but he was having none of it; he splashed the water with his front flippers, gave his cry, and tried to jump out of the pool. Although the water was only six inches from the top, he found this very difficult and it took him a few hours before he finally made it. After that he soon learnt how to hop out.

The following day I lowered Jenny into the pool. She slithered straight in near Flipper, splashed everywhere and the two of them had a good old scrap, but they did not hurt one another. The next problem was how to feed them whilst in the water. They would eat out of my hand, but couldn't yet eat fish thrown into the pool. I had to throw the other seals' fish to the top end, then quickly hand a fish each down to Flipper and Jenny; as I did so they jumped up at it and my fingers nearly went with the fish. Very often people looking at the Sanctuary would ask me questions whilst I was feeding the pups and I had to take care not to have my attention distracted.

The doors to Flipper's and Jenny's pen were left open and, at night, they used to go in on their own. One evening whilst we were in bed, we heard a great clatter in the Sanctuary, so I rushed out to see what was going on. I found that Judy had broken down the door to Fatima's pen and she was in the pool. This was going to be very awkward as she hadn't yet learned to take fish out of my hand.

Next morning I discovered her trying to take down a fish that one of the others had left; finally she succeeded. She had done what Flipper and Jenny couldn't yet do: pick up a fish from the water.

There were now seven seals in the pool and one in the shed. The main thing was to see that each had its fair share and this took some sorting out. Flipper and Kim nearly always jumped out for theirs. Fatima sprawled against the gate about nine feet from where I usually fed the others, so I could see to it that she had her share. That left Judy, Simon, Sally and Jenny in the water. I'd throw a fish to the top end of the pool for Judy, then quickly throw one to Sally and Simon, leaving Jenny close to me giving her first cry which enabled me to drop a fish into her mouth. While all this was going on, Kim and Flipper were around my legs pulling at my trousers and Wellington boots; then Flipper (his cry was terrific, and I think it could be heard at the top of the valley) would keep at me until he had his fair share.

Finally I would go to the pen and feed Blacky who just wouldn't eat on his own. I had once put him into the pool, but he had no idea of taking fish in the water and with all the other seals swimming around, if I threw the fish to him, someone else had it before he could even turn to smell it. When, after two days, he still didn't attempt

A DISASTROUS WINTER

to go for the fish, I had to put him back into the shed as I couldn't leave him long without food.

My time was pretty well occupied. After feeding the seals I got the fish out of the fridge ready for the next feed, and then started looking after our birds. We have twelve small parrots whose cages need to be cleaned out and fresh water and food put in, and then there are the two macaws (Blue and Gold) who need the same attention. Harry and Mac, as they are called, usually say 'Hello' to me, after which I scratch their necks and Mac always wants to come out on to my shoulder, to peck at my ear and pull my hair.

While I was dealing with the birds, out came the badgers from their home-made set. They had been found abandoned while still too young to feed themselves. No doubt their parents had been killed by people who regard badgers as enemies. They were brought to me to be weaned and cared for and then settled in for good. First they sniffed around me. (They recognised my scent; had I been a stranger, their hair would have bristled out like a hedgehog and their heads would have been tucked down low.) Then they went to the tins into which I had scraped the droppings and the food I had cleaned out of the birds' cages. These they pulled over with their thick, strong front legs, and then scratched out all the seed.

During the day the badgers accepted my company, but were not very playful. It was not till ten o'clock in the evening that, even though I had the lights on, they would begin to tear around, pulling at my trousers and jacket and charging to and fro between my legs. This was a regular game that took place each evening and to which they looked forward.

Once they had all been fed, I had to see to the two mynah birds who lived in our house (by now they would both be chattering noisily). They can say almost anything, talking as a rule in the tone of the person who has taught them their words.

One way and another, we now had a large and varied animal family.

CHAPTER ELEVEN

Protection for the Wild Life of our Coasts

IN March 1970 a few sea birds – mostly guillemots – were brought to me with oil on their feathers; not badly oiled, but sufficient to make them waterlogged, so they were either carried in by the current or they made for rocks near the water's edge.

Our beach at St Agnes quickly became a death-bed. There were thirty dead guillemots lying thickly covered with freshly deposited oil, also two gannets and two razorbills. Gannets are large sea birds with long beaks, very similar to young swans. On the rocks I could see about another thirty birds huddling together in little black groups. These proved to be guillemots, the black oil had obliterated the whiteness of their feathers and the grey of their head and wings. The stance of these birds reminds one of penguins and they looked like a group of sad little old men.

I knew it was impossible for me to cope with such a number in my Sanctuary, so I rang the RSPCA Inspector for help and to ask him to make arrangements for them to be taken to the Bird Sanctuary at Mousehole, near Penzance, where the best treatment would be given them.

The Inspector came immediately and that morning we gathered forty guillemots from the beach and the rocks. It was pitiful to see them: the majority were completely plastered and so thick was the oil on their bodies, they could not even run away from us. We got them back to the Sanctuary, transferred them into special boxes and made arrangements for their journey.

Lunch over, we made a trip to Trevellas, another little beach off St Agnes. There we found another ten birds dead and six alive, but badly oiled. Again we found two gannets, this was unusual for during the *Torrey Canyon* disaster when thousands of sea birds lost their lives, only two or three gannets were involved.

Soon birds began to arrive from Perranporth, a few miles away, and then from Newquay. People on the beaches noticed their plight and began collecting them and bringing them to the Seal Sanctuary. During the afternoon, we collected another fifty birds off our own beach, all in a very bad condition. This was serious, but to any outsider watching us, it must have appeared comical; there was the Inspector and myself chasing the birds, who went first one way and then the other, always trying to make for the safety of the open sea. It was necessary for us to catch them quickly before they started preening, for if they did this feather cleaning operation themselves, they would swallow oil which would burn their stomachs and death would be certain. Another hazard was provided by the gulls. The oiled birds were a helpless target and were often attacked and pecked to death by the tougher seagulls.

For the second time in three months my garage was housing distressed sea victims; first the dying baby seals and now the dying sea birds. The ones we knew had no chance of survival, and who were suffering, were put to sleep. By evening, our total of dead and alive birds rose to 163, including eight gannets. We made a final check on the beach as darkness fell: there were still many birds out at sea sitting on the water and we knew that tomorrow would again be a busy day.

At nine o'clock next morning I saw at least twenty birds on the sands; the rocks to the left were obscured from my view, but I guessed there would be as many again sheltering there. By mid-day we had picked up eighty oiled victims. We had covered the three beaches in the St Agnes area, but it was easy to miss birds, especially if they were among the rocks, for the oil acted as camouflage, birds and rocks blending in colour, and also guillemots were apt to wedge themselves in crevices and only the occasional flutter gave away their hiding place.

The beaches were not one mass of oil, as with the *Torrey Canyon*, but small amounts were being deposited by the tide as though they had been separated from a larger slick off the coastline. The winds were strong north-westerly, helpfully washing the birds in. Other areas were sending to us for help, showing that the affected coastline stretched from Newquay to the north of us to St Ives to the south.

The count that evening showed that still another 150 birds had been collected and these included four gannets. By then we were feeling the strain, for one thing our legs were unaccustomed to these miles of walking and sprinting.

Next day we found that overnight more oiled birds had beached themselves. They needed to be picked up. At this point, the Inspector and I realised that to cope with the beaches and to reach all the distressed birds was getting beyond us. An appeal for volunteers to patrol the beaches and to help transport the birds to Mousehole was made on television. Many answered the call.

At present, by English law there is nothing to stop ships depositing oil into the sea outside a limit of three miles off the coast. The captain of a vessel intending to do this may, if he wishes, inform the nearest coastguard station that he is depositing oil from his bilges. What follows is then up to them. In this way the coastline can be polluted, thousands of birds can lose their lives and the ratepayer, through his Council, has to foot the cost of cleaning the beaches. This is surely a most unsatisfactory situation.

Our neighbours were by now taking me for granted and any animal or bird injured, or in difficulty, was brought to me – I was anxious to give all the help I could, but I hadn't enough room to take care of all the casualties properly. So to have the funds to extend the Sanctuary, we thought that the only solution would be to sell our beach business.

We planned a really good filtration plant that would operate three pools, keeping the water perfectly clear and free from bacteria; outbuildings to accommodate sick pups, each room having an infra-red lamp, and besides these we would need an oxygen tent, a surgery room and a deep freeze for storing fish.

All this was going to cost a large sum of money, but if the work were to be carried out properly, it was essential; also it would enable us to make tests on sick seals, from which we would gain more knowledge about how the pups contracted certain diseases, perhaps even, in time, we might be able to help to find a cure for the pneumonic condition, which seems to be one of the main killers.

In December we had had a new problem; all the pups washed in developed ulcers, some had them all over their bodies. Specimens were taken but were not revealing. The other main cause of death was still starvation. Why had so many pups died from it? We had had worse winters than this one, yet nearly a whole generation of baby seals died over a period of two to three months. Was there a lack of small fish? If so, what had happened to them? Or had the mothers gone off to sea and abandoned their babies? If this were the case, what had caused them to do something so unusual? Even if all these pups had lost their lives through natural causes during the average winter weather we had had between September and November, then the next five winters would practically wipe out the seal colonies around the Cornish coast. An estimate of two to three hundred seals is given for Cornish coastal waters, so about seventy to eighty pups would be a fair number to be born in winter.

Mrs Joyce Butler, the M.P. for Wood Green, asked a question in the House of Commons about the recent deaths of seals. But the Minister of Agriculture and Fisheries was only able to reply that the investigation he had ordered to be undertaken by the Veterinary Investigation Laboratory at Truro had found no evidence of contamination by any toxic substance and that the findings had been passed to the Natural Environment Research Council whose Seal Unit had the matter in hand.

The scientists' verdict is that these seals died of starvation, lung congestion and septicaemia, and this is obviously correct, but how can we discover what happened out at sea that caused them to starve? I would like to think that non-recurrent natural causes were responsible since I hope that our advanced techniques in industry are not going to make our sea life suffer and perhaps in time become extinct, as could be the case if the disaster has arisen from pollution.

Land and sea animals have all been given their allotted place on this earth; we know that sometimes certain species have to be thinned out for their own good, as well as for our own benefit, but when sea birds are destroyed in huge numbers, as is the case with oil pollution, then something must be done to control or to stop it.

This story ends in March 1970. Sally and Simon chase each other in and out of the pool; Jenny too has attached herself to Simon so these three have a fine time together, and besides these games each has his individual playtime with me. Fatima and Flipper have paired up, but are a little jealous of my attention to the others.

Judy and Kim have been, and will remain, together as a separate pair; they play with each other, only occasionally teasing their more cumbersome and much slower comrades.

Blacky, who is still in isolation, is improving gradually and we hope he will soon be able to join the rest of the party.

These and the other pups that will surely come to us will need help and if by your small donations you will assist us with their feeding and their treatment and, especially, with the improvements to the Sanctuary, then our work can go on.

Whether the causes of the seals' distress are natural or unnatural, their lives must be saved for their own sake and also because if interest in the wild life of today is not maintained and developed, then none will exist tomorrow.